Your Home Matters

Sue M. Wilson

Open Door Publishing - Hendersonville NC

Published by Open Door Publishing - Hendersonville, NC

www.suemwilson.com

ISBN: 978-0-9991104-1-6

Library of Congress Control Number: 2018901965

Contents

Introduction _____1

Chapter 1: GETTING STARTED: Getting the boost you need_____5

Chapter 2: ENTRANCE: Inviting the Lord's presence into your home _17

Chapter 3: LIVING, FAMILY OR GREAT ROOM:
Abundant living _____23

Chapter 4: MEDIA: Yikes! It's all over the house!_____31

Chapter 5: BEDROOMS: You need to get your rest. _____39

Chapter 6: CLOSETS: Do you really need more? _____51

Chapter 7: OFFICE: Finding what you need, when you need it _____65

Chapter 8: KITCHEN: Where everyone ends up _____75

Chapter 9: FOOD INVENTORY, MEAL PLANNING AND SHOPPING:
Life would be easier if we did not have to eat! _____83

Chapter 10: LAUNDRY:
It seems to multiply when you're not looking! _____101

Chapter 11: BATHROOMS: Clean one in 10 minutes _____113

Chapter 12: GARAGE AND YARD:
Are these areas serving you well?_____121

For Your Consideration _____129

Epilogue _____133

From My Heart_____135

About the Cover
Folly Beach, South Carolina

Only people like Len and me could get excited about the project we were about to embark upon. Our newly purchased property was two blocks from the beach with a main house and two cottages on it, of course, with everything in desperate need of renovation. One of the cottages was covered in foliage so much so that it was hard to find the door! We were fairly sure this cottage would need to be torn down. When we did find the door, we were surprised to see the overgrowth was not confined to just the outside! It was hard to imagine that the previous inhabitant had rented this cottage, in this condition, for more than twenty years! We heard he had a keen interest in horticulture, and that was a good thing because ample vegetation grew everywhere! As we pulled ivy off the ceiling and walls, we surveyed the 500-square-foot structure and started to marvel at the potential of this little home. It was solid through and through. It eventually became our charming little home away from home (and the cover of this book) as we continued to renovate the big house and the other cottage.

Before picture - front of cottage   *Before picture - back of cottage*

For more pictures inside and out go to my website **www.suemwilson.com**

Dedicated to my Mom Madeline Curtis –
she always made home a place I wanted to be –

I miss you…

Acknowledgements

I would like to thank JoAn Blackmon for planting the seed that grew into the first Your Home Matters class and eventually this book. Thanks go out to all Your Home Matters class participants, you made teaching so much fun! To Andi Ball – I appreciate your willingness to apply my book in its rough stages as we worked (long distance) on some of your home matters. Your insight and suggestions have been implemented throughout this book. I am grateful to all who have prayed for me during this process – you know who you are!

Saving the best for last, I want to thank my husband Len for making my dreams come true, and writing this book is one of them. Doing life with you becomes better and better as we continue to encounter one adventure after another...

And finally, I thank The Lord Jesus Christ for giving me the desire in my heart to be an encourager.

Introduction

Dear Reader,

How I wish we were getting to know each other over cups of coffee! There is nothing I would rather do than get to know you and what matters most to you in your home. This book will give me an opportunity to share with you, and as you navigate through each chapter I hope that you will share with me about your home! After the epilogue in the section titled From my Heart you will see my website address, where you can contact me.

To think it all started with an income tax return! In the first year of our marriage, my husband Len had the daunting task of preparing our income tax return and needed to fill in my occupation. He listed me as a "housewife." As I looked at that, I thought, at least he had not filled in "none" or "does not work." He already knew that the discrepancy between the perception and the reality of working in the home was a sore spot with me and how much I resented the comment, "Oh, you don't work." Although I did not have a job outside of our home, I worked—all the time it seemed. But I must admit that I did not like my occupation being described as a "housewife" either. I was married to my husband, Len, not my house! I soon realized and began to verbalize that I was a "homemaker"! Over the years I have heard terms like "household engineer" and even "domestic goddess," but I think I will stick with "homemaker"; it more accurately describes what I want my job to be all about. I was in the business of making our house a home, truly a challenging task in some of the places we have lived!

I was asked by a pastor in my church if I would consider teaching a class about our homes. She asked me because she encountered women on a regular basis who were struggling with basic home-related skills. This caused them so much stress that they could not even consider their homes as places they could enjoy. I already had a different subject in mind, but teaching about our homes excited me!

The outline came together quickly for a course I would call *"Your Home Matters."* This class was one of fourteen offered at Morning Grace, a large weekly ministry our church offers to women in our community. I have had the privilege of teaching it several times to women of all ages over a period of three years — and I can't wait to teach it again! Teaching this class brought me great joy as I watched confidence build in the women who were learning to manage and enjoy their own homes.

Reaching now beyond the classroom, I am offering this book to you to encourage, instruct, and share with you what I have learned and experienced. Creating a home that glorifies the Lord and making the home-front "top priority" can change your family dynamics more than anything else. Comments and real-life examples are included throughout the book to remind you that you are not alone in this endeavor.

An important component of this book is inviting God into our homes and the management of them. He truly does care about what concerns us. Something wonderful happens when our everyday life and our love for God merge. We realize that we never have to feel alone. I hope you discover that Jesus is interested in every detail of your life and your home, and that you can invite Him into your mess — no matter where it is! So if reclaiming your home and filling it with peace, joy and the presence of God interests you, I think you will enjoy this component of the book. The Scriptures I have included throughout the book are mostly from the New Living Translation, which is one of my personal favorites. If the Scripture reference is from another translation, that will be noted in parenthesis.

Home management is not easy. When clutter and disorganization get the upper hand, stress is sure to follow. You may be the type of person who likes to have everything out where you can see it; there is a way to do that in an organized fashion. Maybe you are the extreme opposite; there is a way to keep things put away without becoming obsessive about it, or perhaps you find yourself somewhere in-between the two. *Your Home Matters* is designed to help you discover what will work for you, right where you are, with what you have. You will experience the added benefits of lowering your stress level and keeping more money in your pocket as well as learning simple ways to keep your home organized and clean. But most important of all, you will learn how to make your home a peaceful and enjoyable place where you will want to be and even want to share with others!

Some of my friends refer to themselves as the CEOs of their homes. Maybe you have never considered homemaking in that light before, but that is a pretty good job description! Like companies that develop their core values and articulate them in their mission statements, you will have the opportunity to do that too. Crafting a mission statement for your home will help you see and communicate to your family and others what is most important to you. To help you get started, I will share some examples from participants in a *Your Home Matters* class. Some women have even framed their mission statements and placed them in a central location, providing a constant reminder of what they want their homes to be about.

Practical tips and tricks of the trade that really work: we all love them! I have included some of my favorites; I really use them! Some are original, and many I have discovered through close friends and friends I'll never personally know. Thanks to you, my life is easier and my job more enjoyable and fun.

In my forty-year (and counting) vocation of making a home, I have been blessed to have had others encourage me along the way. It is my privilege to do that for you, cheering you on in all of your home matters. I extend to you an invitation to relieve your stress and love your home, because - *Your Home Matters!*

In the next chapter

As promised, you will fill out a stress and assessment evaluation where you will rate each room or area of your home according to your current level of stress. I will also introduce you to the easy-to-implement system that will not only get you started, but also keep you going! Crafting a mission statement for your home will be explained with some examples given. This will spur you on in creating your own. Let's get started!

Chapter 1

———⟡———

Getting Started
Getting the boost you need

Scripture

Commit everything you do to the Lord. Trust him, and he will help you.
~ Psalm 37:5

Bringing organization to your home through the decluttering process can be a daunting task. This chapter will give you the boost you need to help you start and keep you going. You will meet head-on what to do when you feel overwhelmed. You will learn a simple system that really works. But before we get to that, perhaps you can relate to the comment I most commonly hear, "I don't know where to start." It is easy to stall and feel like giving up before you even begin decluttering! If you are willing to commit yourself to the process and ask the Lord to help you, you will find lasting success in bringing order and peace to your home.

"It is a cinch by the inch and hard by the yard." We know this statement is true, but most of us want our homes clutter-free and organized overnight! Overwhelming tasks are manageable when you take small bites; this will keep you from giving up. I want to help you discover what works for you. A by-product of managing your own home efficiently is confidence. Getting a handle on the best way for you to manage constant clutter will give you that confidence and also provide a home that you will enjoy living in. There is no shortage of great ideas for your home, but often those ideas can become distractions from the real task at hand: decluttering! It is easier to implement fun ideas and decorating after you have organized an area. This is a good reward or motivation for you, once the hard work is done. Another concept to put into practice is to "eliminate and concentrate." By eliminating the mess and concentrating on the rest, you will experience how having "less is best" — and much easier to manage and maintain!

I would like to invite you to evaluate your home by taking a stress test — relax; we are not headed for the treadmill, although you might feel like you are getting a work-out! Your home evaluation will help you identify the season of life you are currently in, what you enjoy most about your home and what you don't. The evaluation test is designed to help you define the areas in your home that stress you the most. These areas are good places to start, because you will gain the most benefit there. In those areas of your home that are working for you, the ones that you rate low on your test, keep doing what you are doing! The intention of this book is to reduce your stress, not to make more work for you! If your stress level is similar in most areas, you might want to travel room by room as the chapters are laid out in this book. If your kitchen and laundry area are off the charts, be encouraged: there will probably come a time when you will be cooking and laundering for fewer people. (This possibility was hard for me to even imagine when I was up to my neck in dirty dishes and laundry!)

After you have read about "The System" and rated your rooms, I would encourage you to officially start with the entrance of your home (Chapter 2). Because the entrance is not really a room, decluttering and beautifying this area are fairly easy. Starting here will allow you to become familiar with how The System works on a smaller scale. And you will enjoy the fruits of your labor every time you enter your home!

Stress Evaluation & Assessment

Take your time in answering these questions, and then indicate the stress level in each room of your home. Your answers will help you to define your current living situation and how you feel about your home. I realize that you might be tempted to rate each area high if you are having an overwhelming day. If you feel that way, why not take the test when you can evaluate more accurately? Your honest evaluation will serve you well in helping you know where you want to start decluttering, organizing and making that area of your home serve you better. This assessment and evaluation will also help you see which areas are already working for you.

Home Assessment Questions

- How would you describe your home: starter home, dream home, temporary home, etc.?
- Who presently lives in your home with you / with whom are you living?
- What is your favorite area of your home? Why?

An interesting observation: Most of us choose as our favorite a room or area that is fairly well-organized, uncluttered and/or nicely decorated — a room we enjoy being in. The good news is, as you progress through this book, you will gain more "favorites." I encourage you to re-evaluate after the decluttering process is completed. You will be amazed!

Stress Evaluation

Rate your stress level: 1 = low – 5 = high

Entrance areas & front porch
  ○ 1 ○ 2 ○ 3 ○ 4 ○ 5

Bedrooms
Yours
  ○ 1 ○ 2 ○ 3 ○ 4 ○ 5
Kids'
  ○ 1 ○ 2 ○ 3 ○ 4 ○ 5
Guest (if applicable)
  ○ 1 ○ 2 ○ 3 ○ 4 ○ 5

Living room
  ○ 1 ○ 2 ○ 3 ○ 4 ○ 5

Family room
  ○ 1 ○ 2 ○ 3 ○ 4 ○ 5

Media room or general
  ○ 1 ○ 2 ○ 3 ○ 4 ○ 5

Office area
  ○ 1 ○ 2 ○ 3 ○ 4 ○ 5

Closets (generally)
  ○ 1 ○ 2 ○ 3 ○ 4 ○ 5

Specific closet(s) _____
  ○ 1 ○ 2 ○ 3 ○ 4 ○ 5

Kitchen and dining area
  ○ 1 ○ 2 ○ 3 ○ 4 ○ 5

Meal planning & preparation
  ○ 1 ○ 2 ○ 3 ○ 4 ○ 5

Laundry
  ○ 1 ○ 2 ○ 3 ○ 4 ○ 5

Bathrooms
  ○ 1 ○ 2 ○ 3 ○ 4 ○ 5

Specific bathroom (s) _____
  ○ 1 ○ 2 ○ 3 ○ 4 ○ 5

Yard & garage
  ○ 1 ○ 2 ○ 3 ○ 4 ○ 5

Cleaning & maintenance
  ○ 1 ○ 2 ○ 3 ○ 4 ○ 5

The System

I want to share with you a basic system that many people use for organizing. You may be familiar with it, or maybe it's new to you. The best part about this system is that it works and can be applied to any room or area of your home. As you begin the decluttering process, you will sort everything into at least three categories: things to throw away; things to give away; and things to store/put away. I can still feel overwhelmed with an area I am trying to declutter until I remember this system. Then I feel instant relief because I know I have a workable plan!

Here is your supply list:
- garbage bags
- 3 or more boxes (size-related to estimated volume)
- painter's tape & marking pen
- index cards, pencil & small box (optional)

You will use your garbage bags for anything that needs to be thrown away or recycled (you can use a box for this too, if you want). The boxes will be used for the other categories (give away, put away) and for items that you are not sure about. Any kind of box will work for this. If you are storing several boxes, use ones that are uniform in shape and stack easily. I prefer the boxes used for file folders. The handles on the sides make lifting easy, and they stack nicely. You could also use laundry baskets for the sorting process; they are easily moved from room to room and might be something you already have.

Another name for the decluttering process is "purging." The verb to purge means to remove something that is undesirable. Undesirable items can be ones that you are not using—and we all probably need to get rid of some of those! It is easy to collect things you think you need or want and then end up not using them. They are taking up valuable space where you could put items you are using. When you are purging, remember to only get rid of items that you actually own—make sure they haven't been borrowed! If you have borrowed items, create a box and mark it "Items to be returned". Even if you have had the item so long that you thought it was yours, even if you are tempted to think that the owner has perhaps forgotten about it, swallow your pride and return it anyway. Take care of that right away by putting the items in your car today! I loaned a book to a friend I didn't remember buying. I was pretty embarrassed when we opened it and saw another friend's name in it! Fortunately the owner was glad to pass it on.

Here are some questions to help you in your decisions on what to purge:
- How often do I use this?
- Do I love it? Or does someone else think I love it? (Many collections start this way!)
- Does this item bring me true and lasting benefit?

Back to the dictionary for a minute: the definition of benefit is something that has a good effect or promotes well-being. Clutter seems to have the extreme opposite effect!

Throw away

Throw away anything that is obviously trash and cannot be recycled. Trash is anything that is broken and you cannot fix, as well as those bits and pieces whose purpose and function have been long since been forgotten. If this is hard for you, thinking you might need those bits and pieces someday, you can toss them all in a box marked with that name. Go ahead and throw out all those keys that go to who-knows-which locks, unless you are willing to try them in every lock. If you absolutely cannot part with the keys, add them to your "bits and pieces" box. Did you know that purging can energize YOU? This process is not an easy one; it is hard work, but you should start feeling really good once you get started!

Give away

There are many places that will take your gently used items; some of these companies will even pick them up from your home. Ask friends and neighbors or check local charities for drop-off/pick-up information. You might consider consigning your items; again, ask around to see what your best option might be. Refrain from donating anything that you know you should throw away; only give away things that still have use.

Some clothing needs to go into a rag bag, saved for your next painting project, or put in the trash. You can remove buttons or embellishments before you toss the item, as long as you have use for them. Be sure to store these where you can find them, maybe with your sewing or craft supplies. Once I have a load to donate, I put it in my car (front seat) and drop it off the next time I am out. This final step really helps the process move along, and I enjoy the feeling as I drive away one load lighter!

Put away

Putting things away is a constant process because people just don't put things back where they belong! "A place for everything and everything in its place" is not just a nice saying. Resist the temptation to lay things down anywhere. Anywhere becomes everywhere, and before you know it clutter is out of control again. It is easier to keep things put away once you have established places for them. Implementing this principle will save you hours, perhaps years, over your lifetime of not having to look for things and is key to winning the war against clutter. I was going to say "key to living clutter-free," but that's not possible! Life is messy and constantly needs to be cleaned up, and everyone encounters clutter that needs to be dealt with on a daily basis. If you have perfectionist tendencies, realizing that clutter is common should help you feel less frustrated and more normal. Another thing to consider when putting things away is to group items or things that you use together. This will make finding what you need easier and help you get a job done faster. When you are working on a project that you know will take you some time to finish, gather your items and keep them together until your project is done. Then replace your tools and supplies where they normally belong, so you will be able to find them when you need them again.

Items to store
(And those things you are not sure about!)

These are the items that you think you might still have use for. This is a tricky category because during the purging process it is easy to either keep things that you really don't need or give away something that you should have kept. This is really not as bad as it sounds; I have done both! You can always get rid of something later when you realize that you really don't need it. And it is well worth the paring-down effort, even if you have to repurchase something that you should have kept. Too many times we hang on to something "just in case" we might need it, someone in our family might need it, or we might meet someone who might need it! There is nothing certain about the word "might"; just take a deep breath and let it go.

Place occasionally used items in a box and store the box on a top shelf of a closet or a cupboard. Be sure to mark the category on a strip of painter's tape adhered to the box. You can also mark the category and contents on a 3 x 5 index card — or do both. I like to use painter's tape because it is easily removed and (usually) does not damage the box. The contents card can be attached to the box with painter's tape or placed with other cards in a small file box. If you are storing a large number of boxes, you can use correlating numbers for your boxes and cards. Storing the boxes numerically in a storage area or garage makes retrieval easier. To find an item, locate the card and match the number on the card with the number on the box, and you'll have the right box to locate the item that you need!

Can't decide?

There will probably be some items that you really are not sure about. Place them in a box with a question mark on it. You could also write the contents on the box/card in the same way I just mentioned. Mark your calendar to review the contents of your box(es) or read through the card(s) in a few months. How do you feel about those items now? If you still are not sure, review in a few more months — as long as you have the space to store the box. You might ask a trusted friend for help with those items you are having difficulty parting with. She or he can help you identify if your attachment is a healthy one.

A good rule of thumb for memorabilia is to designate one box per family member and keep only what fits into that box. This forces everyone to choose what means the most to him or her. As I have gotten older, I have pitched items that I do not want my children to have to deal with. This might seem radical, but one day I tossed my high school yearbooks. I had just heard about friends who had had to go through all of their mom's things after her passing. This got me thinking: would my kids want to keep these or even look at them? I had not opened them once in our forty-plus years of marriage and had moved them too many times to count — even to Australia and back! This is my example and may be something you would never even consider. For those of you who might be feeling bad for me: don't — I still have all of my high school pictures.

Now you know about The System that I will refer to throughout this book. As you can see, it is not a complicated process, although it is hard work! You will find that it will become easier the more you use it. You might consider asking a friend to join you in your decluttering and organizing process. You can encourage and also be accountable to each other — and don't forget to celebrate when you both complete an area of your home.

Pardon me if I repeat this a few times throughout this book: seriously consider declaring a moratorium on buying anything during your decluttering process. The last thing you and I need is more stuff! Learning not to buy on impulse (even if it is a great deal) will save you a lot of money and help you to develop healthy spending habits. Making do with what you have is discovering how to be resourceful. This lost art is making a comeback — and feels good. Rewarding yourself with "well thought out" purchases after you have completed decluttering and organizing an area might be good motivation for you.

Crafting a Mission Statement for your home

Although there are many types of companies we can go to for different services, we find common elements in their customer-service endeavors. Most businesses, whether they are a car dealership, a restaurant or a Fortune 500 company, post a Mission Statement. Here companies express how they intend to conduct business, what their core values are, and what they offer you as their customer. In a similar vein, I encourage you to develop a Mission Statement for your home to express its core values. Take some time to think about what you would like your home to be like—to feel like—and then write it down. In theory the process is quite simple, but it does take time to determine what your core values are and then to craft them into a statement. I have found it helpful to look back to key elements in my childhood home that I either want to duplicate or not. (I hope you join me in realizing that no one grew up in a perfect home; there is no such thing! I once saw a humorous tee-shirt a woman was wearing that said, "I am the FUN in dysfunction." Although dysfunction is no laughing matter, it does us good to realize that it is in all of our families to some degree.) For those undesirable characteristics you might have experienced, select adjectives that describe the opposite behavior and add them in your statement.

Here are some examples:
- gentleness instead of harshness
- peace instead of strife
- the positive instead of the negative
- acceptance instead of rejection
- forgiveness instead of un-forgiveness
- confidence instead of competition

On the positive side, I remember a lot of laughter in my home growing up, and I have included that in my Mission Statement. My parents were older when they had me, with both my sister and brother about to leave the nest. I realize now that most of their stressful years were behind them by the time I came along! I learned from both my mom and my dad that there is always a story to share and something to laugh about. Sometimes that meant being able to laugh at yourself!

Some of the characteristics most of us would enjoy having describe our homes are found in the Bible, especially in Galatians 5:22–23. These characteristic are known as the "fruit of the Spirit." They are love, joy, peace, patience, kindness, goodness, faithfulness, gentleness and self-control.

Here are two examples of home mission statements; the first one is mine.

May all who enter our home feel welcome, loved and accepted.
Let our home provide a refuge ~ a safe place to feel comforted and comfortable.
May all who enter sense the joy of the Lord and be encouraged to laugh a lot.
Let each one who enters find true peace ~ God's peace.

Here is (my daughter in-law) Cara's:

Pray often (always).
Find your identity in Christ.
Show the same grace to others as God has shown you.
Be first to say sorry.
ENCOURAGE OTHERS... LOVE OTHERS.
Always be ready to dance. Laugh until tears are running down your leg!
Hug each other (daily).
BE KIND ~ LISTEN ~ NO YELLING, KICKING OR ELBOWING!
Be thankful.
Always be looking for ways to serve others.
Fill the house with music — worship.
LIVE outside your comfort zone. Be fully dependent on Christ.

I hope you feel inspired and excited to create a Mission Statement for your home. If you are not, would you consider it while you are reading *Your Home Matters?* Remember, your statement will be unique to you and your family. If you keep it honest and heartfelt, it will impact your family as you endeavor to live it out.

The Scripture verse for this chapter is one you will want to keep handy throughout the process of decluttering your home. It is essential to have the Lord's help, strength and wisdom as you move from stress and mess to peaceful success!

Class Comment

As I read over the family mission statement I created, I am very happy with it and peace rushes over me. I notice that there is no mention of being clean or tidy or everyone helping out around the house. Instead it was a structure of purity and a cleanliness of heart, mind and soul that I wish to instill upon my family. It makes you think twice about what your dream home should "look like"; instead, it should be about what our dream home "feels like." I have now printed my mission statement and framed it in our main hallway.

~Krys

In this chapter I hope you answered (or plan to answer) the home and assessment questions and rated each room/area of your current home on the stress evaluation chart (both are on page 6 and 7). I shared a simple and successful system that can be followed throughout the entire decluttering process, and every time you need to declutter again. I promise this will be much easier after the initial decluttering process! You were also encouraged to start crafting a mission statement for your home.

In the next chapter

Easy ways will be discovered to improve the look of entrances into your home. The ideas you gather will make these busy areas serve you and your family better. You will discover ways to save time and money by using things you already have. Not only that – once you tackle these areas of your home, you be able to get out of the house in record time! You can do this!

Chapter 2

Entrance
Inviting the Lord's presence into your home

Scripture

Look! I stand at the door and knock. If you hear my voice and open the door, I will come in, and we will share a meal together as friends.
~ Revelation 3:20

In this chapter you will find help in:
- improving the look of the entrance (s) to your home
- making this busy area serve you and your family
- saving time and $$ by using things you already have

I realize that there are probably other areas that could use your immediate attention, but I am glad you are here. One of the best advantages of starting with the entrance to your home is that you will become familiar with how The System works on a smaller scale. Because this area is not a room, you can manage it without too much effort and usually complete it within an hour or two. If there are several members of your household, your most-used entrance area may take longer to organize. The front door might not be an area you think about, but that is the first place people see—unless they are your back door friends. You might be surprised at what you find on your porch if you rarely use the front door—like a newspaper collection, door knob advertisements, old flower pots with dead plants in them, toys, and spider webs. If you have toddlers, you might find some of those items you thought were lost forever!

"Curb appeal" is a term used by builders and realtors, which refers to the impression your home offers from the street. Paying extra attention to this area will make you smile every time you see it, and it will really pay off when trying to sell a home.

You may have one or two entrance areas: the front door and maybe a back door. Making entrance areas functional will save you both time and money. Time is saved when you don't have to look for things, and money is saved when you don't have to replace those items!

Ready to start?

Let's try out The System (Chapter 1)…

1. Grab 2 trash bags, 2 boxes, a broom, dust pan, and wet rag and head for the area outside your front door. Using the system, throw away and recycle the obvious. Place other items that do not belong there in the "put away" box. Then place anything you do not want in a box to give away. By clearing this area it will be easier to clean and keep clean. You can always add decorative items later.

2. Start from the top and work your way down; knock down spider webs with your broom as you go. You can also dust the ledge over your door with the broom. Dust off any furniture and then sweep the floor area. You might want to grab the hose and spray everything down. I do this periodically or after a storm, because this is where I enjoy starting my day whenever I can, with a cup of coffee and my Bible.

3. Take your wet rag (you might want to use a bucket filled with warm water and a little soap) and wipe down your front door, especially around the handle, and clean any glass.

4. Dump any dead bugs out of your light fixture, and carefully clean it. Use caution: if you break the globe, it might be hard to find a replacement— spoken with the voice of experience. Replace the light bulb if necessary. If you use a lower wattage that lights the area but is not glaring (60 watts is usually recommended), your front door will feel more inviting.

5. Wash or sweep off your door mat. Caution: never use WD-40 or something like Armor All to make it shine. I did this and it looked great, but I went sliding the first time I stepped on it!

6. Critically look at your entrance area, and evaluate if you like the way it looks.

Front porch

If you decide you want a change, try moving things around or adding something to make this area nicer and more inviting. Check out what you already have before purchasing anything. Chances are you'll find something that will work great; it might just need a fresh coat of paint.

Arranging a seating area will give you a nice place to relax. Place a lamp on a table or add a strand of white lights to a wreath or to an existing arrangement and you have created a pleasant ambiance with little effort. Pots of flowers add color and beauty without much investment. Use caution here and only have them if you will remember to water them! You can create your own yard art by finding something of interest to tuck among your flowers, making this area fun and inviting. Before purchasing furniture for your porch, use something you already have first. Then you can get a feel for what you can do with the area. You might be surprised and like it so much that you won't have to buy anything!

For a final touch, add a wreath to your door. You could either make one or buy one for general purpose and then change your flowers / decoration to coincide with the season or an occasion. For a birthday celebration, you could add a party hat or balloons; for patriotic holidays, add a few little flags—I think you get the idea. Several *Your Home Matters* class participants commented on how much fun they had making or adding a wreath or decoration to their front door; they even shared their photos in class.

Now let's move to the other points of entry of your home: inside the front and back doors.

Front entrance

Apply the system to both these areas; throw away/recycle, put away, and give away. If your front entrance is not an area that you use every day, you can make it nice and it should stay that way. If this is a heavily trafficked area, you can refer to the section on the back entrance for ideas and suggestions.

Consider adding size-appropriate furniture like a bench, desk or small cabinet to this area. (Make sure there is enough room to enter comfortably.) This is a good place for a mirror, or a lamp, and family photos.

———————————◆———————————

In some homes you are encouraged to remove your shoes as you enter; if that is the case in your home, providing a chair or place to sit is a considerate touch. You could also have a decorative basket to keep shoes in; this is highly recommended for the entrance area you use most often. You could even provide cozy pull-on type slippers for people to wear once they have removed their shoes!

———————◆◆◆———————

We will talk about your coat or entrance closets specifically in the closet chapter (Chapter 6), but if you are feeling extra ambitious, go ahead and clean that out while you are working in this area. After you have successfully used The System in that closet, only replace the items you are currently using. Storing out-of-season coats elsewhere will make your closet less cluttered. Hang an over-the-door pocket storage system, and you now have a place for those items you use every day and can grab them as you go out the door: hats, gloves, sunglasses, etc.

I keep a basket near my entry and place items I want to give or return to people who I know will be coming to my home soon—items like a book, magazine, recipe, etc. If my adult children happen to come by when I am not home, I can easily direct them to that area to retrieve what I have for them. (I like using baskets in many areas of my home because they are decorative and easily accessed. Baskets are less expensive yard sale items, but before you buy, look to see what you already have or use a box until you find just the right basket.) Your entry is also a great place to keep encouraging sayings, Scripture cards, or candy in a little dish, ready to share.

Back entrance

Whichever entrance has the most traffic will need the most attention. It has probably also become a "catch all" for all kinds of things. To make this area serve you better, concentrate on functionality. After you have successfully applied the System, think about who uses this door. (Hint: Whose belongings consistently find their home there?) You can provide a cubby, basket or bin for each family member in this area. Why not use boxes until you find something else? If your kids decorate and personalize their boxes with paint, paper or magazine pictures, they will be more likely to use them. You may decide that you do not want to replace them! Have everyone place what he or she needs for the next day in his or her box/ bin and your exit will be a breeze.

A dear friend has on occasion placed a box on the floor of her entry closet, where she keeps treasures she no longer wants. She offers them to her guests as they are leaving her home. This makes saying good bye just as much fun as saying hello and keeps her clutter on its way out! (*Thanks for the tip, Charlotte!*)

Placing a bench with hooks above it makes a great place to take shoes off and hang coats or backpacks. This is also a good place to keep your keys, either on a hook or in a bowl or basket. Twisting cup holder hooks into the bottom of a wooden plaque or small black board will give you a neat place to hang keys. If you can get into the habit of placing them there, you won't lose valuable time looking for them. This might be a good place to charge your electronic devices too.

Placing a black board here will provide a fun way for family communication. Use black board paint and you can transform many interesting objects into writable surfaces. Try painting on the glass of a picture frame. You could even paint a baking pan, or the inside or outside of a cabinet door.

Once you have decluttered and provided a place for your things, you will see how easy and nice it is to come home, put your things away, and find them again the next day!

Maintenance – Keeping it tidy

Because this is a high-traffic area, applying The System along with your routine cleaning will keep the points of entry to your home functioning well. If this area still seems to "collect" an abundance of items on a regular basis, provide appropriate containers or baskets and groups like items together—maybe a garbage can too!

In this chapter I hope the scripture encourages you to take some time and invite the Lord's presence into your home. It's an easy thing to do. Stand on your porch (not necessary, but the experience will amaze you) and in your own words invite the Lord's presence in, because after all, he is knocking! You also learned easy tips to make each entrance of your home serve you and your family better!

> *Look! I stand at the door and knock. If you hear my*
> *voice and open the door, I will come in, and we will*
> *share a meal together as friends.*
> ~ Revelation 3:20

In the next chapter:

You will find help sorting through all the "stuff" that ends up in your living room, and learn easy ways to create space for each family member's relaxation. I will provide helpful tips on how to stay ahead of the mess and create fun times with your family. Let's create comfy places we can keep clean and organized in no time at all!

Chapter 3

Living Room, Family or Great Room
Abundant living

Scripture

My purpose is to give them a rich and satisfying life.
~ John 10:10b

In this chapter you will find help in:
- sorting through all the "stuff" that ends up in here
- creating space for each family member's relaxation
- keeping a step ahead
- creating family fun time

Life is the most messy
where you spend most of your time!

The living room can be referred to as the great room, gathering room, or family room. It really does not matter what you call it, life happens here. Because life is messy, this room can be one of the messiest of all! Take heart: great times can be enjoyed without all the clutter, and it is not impossible to keep this area in good form, functional and fun!

The "front room" was the name for this area in my home when I was growing up. That was because we entered it from the front of the house, at the front door. Our couch, coffee table, end tables, lamps and one and only television were the furnishings of this room. We also had some built-in book shelves for our small collection of books. I can distinctly remember hearing my mother say, "Susan, would you please sit down!" as I annoyed my parents by parking myself right in front of the television. I did have a problem sitting still. Today it is rare for all of the family to gather in one area; we tend to spread out more. There is value in both, but it will take some strategic planning to bring a family together, and this is a great room to do that in!

At the turn of the 19th to the 20th centuries some homes had a parlor or sitting room. My guess is that because they were set apart from other areas of the home, they probably stayed fairly tidy. Not only years have passed since then, we have also collected more possessions than ever. I would like my living room to not look so lived in! There is a way to do that, providing both a place for family to relax and a fairly orderly place to enjoy coffee with friends.

Did you rate this room as a high or low stress area on the stress evaluation in Chapter 1? In answering a few questions, you will be able to define the functions of this area for your home. If you have more than one living room area, answer the questions for each area.

- What is in this room?
- What do you want to use this room for?
- What belongs in this room?
- Is there anything in this room that you wish was not here?

Ready to start?

With the purpose of this area now defined, be ruthless as you apply The System found in Chapter 1! As you roll up your sleeves, remember that you want to transform this room into an area that serves you well. During the decluttering process, grab a basket or container for each family member's belongings that you find and that are no longer welcome here! Encourage everyone to be responsible for the items in his or her basket by throwing away, putting away or giving them away. You are resourcing them with valuable life skills if you teach them how to use The System. When you are finished, replace only the items that you really want.

Furniture placement

If your room is in a "high traffic" area, your furniture arrange-ment needs to be strategic. You can define space and where you want traffic to flow with how you arrange your furniture and place your rugs. Think about conversation and coziness too, while you are at it. This can be as easy as pulling your couch away from the wall and placing chairs close by. If you want to float your couch and chairs in the middle or at the edge of a room, place a rug just in front of your couch to make it look right. Taking a minute to sit in each chair will help you know how you need to place them. I like to look at room arrangement in magazines or online to give me ideas on how to make my room look great.

Ideas to keep this area under control and functional

- Find a basket or container to house remote controls and maga-zines. Use one that looks nice and from which items can easily be retrieved.

- Use the lower shelves of your bookcase for kids' or pets' toys or for other items you want to keep handy. Place these items in a basket too, adding a decorative touch.

- Stacking some of your books and placing something that catch-es your eye on top adds interest and allows you to enjoy your treasures in a new way. If you have a lot of "treasures," rotating them, instead of having all of them out at once, will keep dusting to a minimum.

- If you need to move the items off your coffee table periodically to play games, etc., place them on a decorative tray; this is easy to move and will keep your table looking tidy.

- Stack "coffee table" books with a correlating object on top, such as a large shell on top of Oceans of the World or a framed picture of your travels on top of a travel book. For a book on coins, place a small basket with special coins on top.

Pillows

New pillows are an inexpensive way to change your room. You can easily cover a pillow, without sewing, by wrapping some material around it, turning the edges under for a clean finish, and tying a scarf or ribbon around it to keep the material secure. You can also wrap a scarf around a pillow, tying it with a knot or a bow. Add a little bling with a glitzy pin you never wear to the center of a pillow.

For a fresh look

You can change out your wall hangings or re-hang one you already have at eye level. Slip covers are a good way to make your couch or chair look new.

Framing

Photos warm up any room and can be enjoyed every day, unlike those in albums. Collages are also fun: find photos from many places with a common theme, like doors, gates, flowers, etc. If you have a collection of mismatched frames, paint them all the same color to create a nice effect.

Hang it!

Tapestries can be hung in various ways and can cover large areas; you could even hang some interesting fabric. A creative friend did this with a cool-looking skirt she no longer wore. She framed a section of her skirt and now has quite a conversation piece — and enjoys her skirt in a new way! Thanks Josie!

Creating family fun

- If you want to direct your family away from the television, keep your board and card games easily accessible. If your children are still not interested, play the game with them! One of my most treasured childhood memories is of my Aunt Maxine playing games with my cousins and me.

- You can spare yourself all… of… that… card-sorting by organizing the number of card decks you need for each of the games you like to play. I like to band them together along with game instructions so we're ready to go!

- Create an area to put together puzzles by placing a card table in the corner of the room. Try to choose an area that has good lighting. Working on large jig-saw puzzles provides an excellent opportunity for family time and will create a sense of accomplishment as you see the picture coming together. Making a space for this also allows you the luxury of leaving the puzzle out and working on it over a period of time.

- To encourage more reading, provide materials that are age-appropriate for every family member.

- Place small craft projects on a book shelf in a basket, along with all of your materials, and you will have something fun to do on a rainy day.

- Designate specific areas to watch television, play video games, and read, to make your room multi-functional.

- I like to keep my Bible- study material all together in a basket, therefore keeping my time from being interrupted by having to hunt for a pen, journal, etc.

Item of interest

To make reading, playing trivia games and watching television or movies more interesting, provide a world globe, map or atlas in your room. This will connect you to the area you are learning about.

Maintenance — Keeping it tidy and organized!

If you hate to dust, a feather duster really speeds up the process because you can dust over items without moving them!

If this area seems to collect various items from family members on a regular basis—like backpacks, shoes, jackets, etc.—and there is no other place for them, a workable solution is to provide stackable decorative baskets, one for each person in your family. Now they can toss their things in that basket instead of on the floor or on the couch. Before dinner or bedtime they will need to be responsible for putting their belongings away. Have them return their baskets to be ready for the next day. If everyone becomes familiar with this process, items are less likely to get lost, and your living room area stays uncluttered.

―――――――◆―◆―――――――

One mother of young children I know likes to keep a hand-held vacuum concealed in her living room so she can clean up crumbs from family snacks quickly.

―――◆―◆―――

In this chapter

I hope these ideas started your wheels turning about how you can make the living room areas of your home more enjoyable, and how you can keep them that way! I love the scripture for this chapter because it reminds me that Jesus' purpose is to give us a rich and satisfying life - not one of surviving, but of thriving!

> *My purpose is to give them a rich and satisfying life.*
> ~ John 10:10b

In the next chapter

Now that we have finished up the living room areas of your home, let's take a look at how we can improve the quality of your living by getting a grip on the various types of media that find their way into our homes! You will be encouraged to choose where you want your media and where you don't as well as creating "media-free" zones. Let's get the family back to the dinner table! And I will tell you how to practically deal with all of those devices and those cords – once and for all!

Your Home Matters

Chapter 4

———⧢———

Media
Yikes! It's all over the house!

Scripture

A house is built by wisdom and becomes strong through good sense. Through knowledge its rooms are filled with all sorts of precious riches and valuables.
~ Proverbs 24:3–4

Fix your thoughts on what is true, and honorable, and right, and pure, and lovely, and admirable. Think about things that are excellent and worthy of praise.
~ Philippians 4:8

In this chapter you will find help in:
- choosing where you want media and where you don't
- creating "media-free" zones
- navigating the family back to the dinner table
- dealing with the practical side
- thinking through the effect of your "choices" of media

When I was growing up, the cutting edge for media included radio, records and color television. I remember feeling pretty cool carrying around my very own baby-blue transistor radio, and I could not wait to get my allowance so I could buy the "number one hit" on a single record each week for only ninety-nine cents! Watching television was more of an event with my family, as we gathered around to watch the Wonderful World of Disney. Sometimes we munched on popcorn and we always laughed a lot. Controlling devices used to be as easy as pushing the on and off buttons. Now we have so many remotes it is no wonder it can take several tries to locate the right one and then several more tries to push the right buttons! (True confession: I am not proficient at this! I have had to call my kids to walk me through operating our television when Len is out of town.)

In this chapter we will talk about where your media live and how to manage them. But, more important, help will be offered in recognizing the enticement of media and living free from their bombardment!

Do you control the media in your home or do they control you?

Television has become more like a constant companion in many homes today. Its continuous din in the background creates a type of white noise of its own, keeping many people company and helping others to fall asleep. If we were to lose or misplace our most used communication device, we would feel like we had lost a limb!

The world of technology is changing daily, and we can't keep up! Do you really need to or want to keep up? Some of you will say "yes," and I am truly in awe of your ability to learn new systems with ease; I wish I was better at that. I have to admit, the media that are available are amazing: never before has the world been so connected. We can know what is happening on the other side of the world in "real time," through "breaking news". Friends and family can be communicated with or prayed for in a matter of minutes through social media. Unfortunately, there is a dark side to most things and media are no exception. Media and raising children have been a breeding ground for contention for generations, but currently they raise more challenges than ever. You may place media restrictions on your children, but they still seem to get exposed to the objectionable. Seeking the Lord for wisdom is essential in navigating and communicating effectively the danger of these types of traps with your kids.

Isn't it amazing how the hours fly by when you are watching television or on the Internet? I remember being the only one who got excited when the electricity would go off when our children were still home. It seemed as if the world was coming to an end when the television would not turn on! After the family adjusted, we would light candles, enjoy an easy dinner, and play board games or talk. I was tempted many times to just unplug the thing, but then I knew I would have to confess that I did know what was wrong with the television, and I did not want to be tempted to lie!

Let's talk about the practical side first.

Location, location, location really is everything, especially when it comes to media placement. We no longer are dealing with a television just in the living room; it is quite common to find one in each bedroom, the kitchen, and sometimes even in the bathroom—and that is just the televisions! In most of our homes "media" are plentiful and widespread, taking up way too much real estate! Even if you have a designated "media room," chances are you can still find bits strewn all over the house.

Planning what media you really want and need is a good place to start. How many televisions? How many computers or video games? You might have a battle on your hands if you want to pare down when televisions are already in every bedroom. Your kids may never thank you if you remove the televisions from their rooms, but please know you are brave for that tough call.

Ready to start?

Using The System (Chapter 1), throw away, give away and put away all media, working your way through each area of your home that needs a "media makeover." This is a great time to get rid of the old relics that still work but you never use. (We have switched to laptops for ease of use, and we like the little space they take up.) As you have done in other areas of the house, place an individual's items that do not belong in common areas in his or her designated box to speed up this process.

Tips for putting things away:

- If this area has become a dumping ground for backpacks, books, etc., provide a decorative bin for each family member. You can store them in an entertainment center or on a bookshelf.

- Corral remote controls in a basket or decorative container and thus provide a permanent place for them to live.

- Apply Velcro to the remote and the side of your wall-hung television; that will keep it handy.

- Transferring your CDs and DVDs to large album-type storage frees up a lot of space because you can eliminate the cases. I have one section in ours for music and one for movies. Just slip the music information folder in with the CD. I also cut the movie information from the case to fit in the album pocket with the movie. Keep a couple of extra cases to put your movies or CDs in for travel or for lending purposes.

- If you lend music, movies or books, maintain a log to help you keep track of who has what.

- You can eliminate the bulk of CDs and DVDs by watching your movies and listening to your music online!

- Game boxes can take up a lot of space and get tattered over the years. You can remove them from their boxes, keeping all of the game parts, directions and board in a sturdy two-gallon zip-type bag. Since the box is already shot, cut out the name of the game and slip that into the bag too, making it visible at a glance. Now you can store all of your game bags in a basket or bin that takes up one third of the space. With your games all together, they can easily travel to the table to play. They will be easier to transport when you want to take them with you on vacation too.

- Cord management becomes necessary with media and in office and desk areas. If you have several things plugged into the same power strip, tag each cord with a plastic bread clip. You can write on the clip before attaching it to identify the cord. Cords can be contained in plastic sleeves purchased from office supply stores and can be painted to match walls, floors, etc.

- Centrally located televisions and computers are always best for children, making it easier to keep a watchful eye.

- One mom in a *Your Home Matters* class placed a power strip on their baker's rack to store her kids' laptops. Supervision was easy, and they looked tidy. If you do not have a baker's rack, grab your tape measure and see what you have around the house to serve the same purpose. (Thanks for the tip, Elizabeth!)

She carefully watches everything in her household.
~ Proverbs 31:27

Navigating your family back to the dinner table...

Even if it is for only a few nights a week, it is well worth the effort to make it happen. Keeping connected with what is really going on in each family member's life is a challenge with our busy schedules! Sitting down together for a meal is the perfect time to institute some "positive" communication. Refrain from using this time to bring correction and discipline; choosing another time for that will keep your family meal time positive and fun. To extend this together time, include the family in meal prep and clean-up. An added bonus: you are teaching them life skills, and you know they won't go hungry when they are out on their own.

Class Comment

Jennifer shared that, with several children in the house and the many activities they were involved in, it seemed impossible for her family to all be together at dinner time. But breakfast worked for them! Each morning they would gather around the table and talk about what each one of them would be doing that day and how they could pray for each other. What a way to start your day!

Here are some ideas to make this a fun and beneficial time for everyone:

- Have each person answer a question randomly pulled from a stash you have made ahead of time. Have your kids write out some of the questions to get them involved.

- Take turns going around the table sharing your "high" and "low" for the day. This will help everyone feel comfortable talking about her or his day and will give insight into what is really happening in everyone's life. Be sure to share about your day too; being transparent about things that won't cause your children to worry is a wonderful way to show them that you need their encouragement and prayers too.

- If you are ready to teach your children basic life skills, have them take turns helping with meal preparation, setting the table and cleaning up. Conversation can start here and continue until the last dish is put away.

Don't just remove — replace!

When my children were small and got a hold of something I did not want them to have, I used to offer them something that they could have. It will take creativity on your part to distract and divert your children away from unhealthy media, but is well worth it. Get your kids involved by asking them what they think will help them learn to make better choices. You might have a fight on your hands, but if you have made up your mind that this will work, it usually does!

Find classic books for them to read or listen to as a family. We spent hours on family road trips listening to Huckleberry Finn on tape. Our now adult children can still quote many of the funny sayings from that classic story. Find age-appropriate games and puzzles—even the most reluctant teen might just surprise you and join in the fun. Crafts are a great replacement for media too; be on the lookout for fun things your family can do together, especially around a holiday. You can enforce time limits and taking turns by using an actual timer for video games. This will help your kids bring balance into their lives and limit their game playing.

Turn on uplifting music to greet your family members as they come home, and you are creating a wonderful atmosphere.

Making quality literature, music and even board games available in your home will bring the discovery of some of the finer things in life, things that are timeless. Share with your family some of the games you played when you were growing up and show them why you liked playing them.

One summer my neighborhood friends and I had continuous Monopoly games going on. Since we could never get any adults to play with us, we played each other almost every day! We loved becoming very familiar with the game and even improved our math skills. I wonder if any of my friends share my interest in real estate and building – or perhaps some have become bankers.

Unplug

Choose a weekend for you and your family to unplug. Pray about it and plan ahead for fun things that you can to do together without any type of media. It's not as easy as it sounds. But this could become a regular event in your home, guaranteed to make some lasting fun memories!

Class Comment

Bonny and her husband kept the internet modem and router in their master bedroom. This was how they set boundaries for their children's use of the internet. At certain times the internet was not available in their home, forcing them to all find something else to do!

Maintenance – Keeping it tidy and organized!

- If your books, magazines, and movie inventory seem to grow too fast, use the principle of "something in – something out".
- Take a little time right before you go to bed to straighten up the area you were in, and you will be glad you did in the morning!
- You can store many of these items electronically, eliminating clutter quickly.

In this chapter

You were reminded that you can take control of the media in your home – and feel empowered doing so. Some practical storage tips were shared to make your life easier after you have finally decluttered all things called media. Here is one of this chapters scripture verses to help motivate you to choose the best for you and your family.

> *Summing it all up, friends, I'd say you'll do best by filling your minds and meditating on things true, noble, reputable, authentic, compelling, gracious – the best, not the worst; the beautiful, not the ugly; things to praise, not things to curse.*
> ~ Philippians 4:8–9 (The Message)

In the next chapter

We will declutter bedrooms – yours, the children's and the guest room. We will also develop a plan to reclaim and keep these areas for rest, creating true retreats, which will improve your quality of life! For an extra bonus – discover ways to get the sleep you need!

Chapter 5

———✦———

Bedrooms
You need to get your rest

Scripture

He lets me rest in green meadows; He leads me beside peaceful streams.
~ Psalm 23:2

*Then Jesus said, "Come to me, all of you who are weary and carry
heavy burdens, and I will give you rest."*
~ Matthew 11:28

In this chapter you will find help in:
- decluttering bedrooms—yours, children's and guest's
- developing a plan to reclaim this area for rest
- creating a true retreat which will improve your quality of life
- discovering how to get the sleep you need
- finding out what God has to say about sleep

What do you see when you walk into your bedroom? Is it conducive to rest, relaxation, sleep, or romance? You might be thinking, how on earth am I supposed to rest in my bedroom when it has become the catch-all for all sorts of unfinished projects? Because we are usually the only ones who spend time in our bedrooms, they can easily become places for things that we want to keep out of sight or do not have a place for! Several people have shared with me that they store boxes they need to go through, even their bills and unopened mail, in their bedrooms. No wonder we have trouble getting the shut-eye we need!

I am sure that you realize that there are many people who are sleep deprived; perhaps you are one of them. If you're not careful, just thinking about that fact can make you lose sleep! Everyone benefits from a good night's sleep; it is an essential component for good health. Spending time to make your bedroom a place you will want to be in will improve your quality of sleep and your quality of life!

Class Comment

Elizabeth and her husband were in the process of adopting another child, a process that can be very stressful. Although they were fairly sure that everything would work out, they knew that one really can't breathe easy until the last of the paper work is signed and processed. Some of this paper work sat on her night stand and seemed to be the last thing she saw at night and the first thing in the morning. Elizabeth felt challenged and wanted to make some kind of a difference in her bedroom, but raising six girls took most of her time and energy. She shared with our class that all she was able to at this time in her life was move all of the adoption papers out of her bedroom. She was amazed at how much difference that one step made in making her bedroom a more restful place.

Ready to start?

Before you apply the system, review these questions to assess and evaluate your bedrooms, and then use your answers to help you determine what you want in your bedroom.

- What is this bedroom room typically used for?
- What belongs in this room?
- What does not belong or you would rather not have in your bedroom?

Apply The System (Chapter 1) to each bedroom you are working on. If you have an abundance of items you need to keep but need to get out of your bedroom (s), consider transporting them to a temporary place like the garage until you can find a permanent home for them. This will help you to stay focused and to resist the temptation to sort through them now. Focus is so important during the decluttering process; learn to resist becoming distracted by clutter in other areas, and you will feel less overwhelmed. I think the best place for you to start is your bedroom. This might seem a little selfish, but it is not. Most people would agree that, when we get a good night's sleep and are well rested, we are giving a gift to all who know us! I recommend that you work on the clothes closets when you tackle the closet chapter (Chapter 6); just keep the doors shut for now!

Your bed

Take the time to make it — right when you get up. Then every time you enter your room, you will smile instead of sigh when you look at your made rather than unmade bed! If you struggle with this, consider using only a duvet as your top sheet and have a minimal amount of pillows. Then all you need to do is pull the cover up, toss your pillows, and your bed is made. As another plus: you will cut down on laundry by laundering the bottom sheet and pillow cases weekly, and the duvet cover monthly. This might be a good choice for a child's or a teen's room.

Box spring & mattress: You may need to replace yours, but maybe you are not able to handle that expense right now. It is better to wait to buy the best mattress you can afford. This is something that you will use every day, and a good quality mattress will last a very long time. In the meantime, there are a few things you can do to improve the comfort of your current bed.

Too firm: place a plush blanket under your mattress pad for an overall softening effect.

Too soft: place plywood between your mattress and box springs for a firmer feel. Staple an old sheet to the wood to protect the material on both the mattress and box spring.

Mattress protection is necessary to keep your mattress fresh and clean for a long time. You can purchase protectors that are water proof, bedbug resistant, and quiet.

Sheets: Be on the lookout for great deals on sheets. Choose a high thread-count for great comfort and durability. Sheets with a high thread-count continue to get softer as you launder them and last for years.

Pillows: Be on the lookout too for great deals on good pillows. If you use pillow protectors, you will extend the life of your pillows while keeping them clean and fresh. Pillow protectors are inexpensive and easily laundered.

Changing out your bed spread or coverlet will transform your room instantly, as will adding a decorative pillow or two. Instead of buying new pillows, wrap a pillow you already have with material, just as you did in the living room. Remember: no sewing needed; just turn the raw edges under and secure with a decorative ribbon. You can make the ones you have look different by tying a scarf or adding a cool, big button or even a brooch to it.

Head board: Creating a new head board will give any bedroom a "lift." Check out some ideas on the internet for some inspiration. You could use an old door, a bookshelf or a chalk board, or cover plywood with padding and then material. You also might want to use old windows, twigs, shutters, picket fencing, or a metal wall hanging for a unique look. For some of these ideas it is easier to mount your head board to the wall instead of the bed. This makes cleaning easier since you need to slide only the bed away from the wall.

Lighting

A good reading lamp encourages reading before bedtime. If you lack table space, try a clip-on type of light or an efficient book light.

A nice touch

If you have the space, creating a cozy reading corner is a delightful addition to any bedroom. Maybe you can grab a comfy chair from another area of your home. It is a bonus if your chair has an ottoman — then you can stretch out! Or consider a wicker or upholstered chaise lounge. Get creative in choosing something for a side table; think out of the box, like stacking vintage suitcases together or using a tall sturdy vase with a round glass on the top. Speaking of boxes, you can even use one covered with a table skirt or material that blends with your room, as long as it is sturdy. Top the covered box with a round glass and you are set! Keep a basket in this area to hold a book you are reading, glasses, and maybe a little chocolate to enjoy when you sneak away to your very own bedroom retreat!

Amenities are an easy way to pamper yourself, and having them close can save you from a bedtime workout. Just after I crawl into my warm, cozy bed, often I am up again to get... maybe it is a glass of water, my book, my glasses, that magazine I wanted to read, a cough drop, aspirin, nail file... and the list goes on and on. By taking a few minutes to round up your most needed/used items and placing them in your night stand or a basket close by will keep you in your cozy bed!

Children and guests will benefit from a decluttered bedroom too!

Children

Have you ever wondered why little children are often found playing with their toys instead of taking their nap? That takes more self-control than they have; it is hard not to play when they can see all of their toys. If that is a problem in your home, placing their toys in another location/room or in the closet, where they are out of sight, will make their bedrooms more conducive to sleeping. When it comes to toys, "less is best!" Fewer toys mean less time spent in clean-up, which will help keep children from feeling so overwhelmed. If you need to pare down the number of toys, consider letting the children choose their favorite items and give the rest away. Are there still too many toys? Put some away and trade them out every few months. See Chapter 6 on closets for more ideas.

Extra steps:

- Personalize items in children's rooms. They will love seeing their names or initials.
- Frame the meaning of their names and remind them that God knows their names.
- Add items to their rooms that they like, e.g., airplanes, particular animals, etc.

Did you know that whatever children consistently look at will make an impact on their lives as adults? What is hanging on their walls? Does it reflect what you want to build into their lives? Is it wholesome? I heard of a family that had a picture in their dining room of a sea captain at the wheel of his ship. Every one of those children grew up loving boats and spent time on the water!

I remember when my kids were teens, I did not always like their choice of posters or how messy their rooms would get. A friend reminded me, "That's what their door is for!" When they were young, I did my best to teach them how to clean their rooms. I have experienced that part of raising children is teaching them to become independent of me, and one way they can do that is having their bedrooms how they like them. I want to encourage you to "prayerfully" choose your battles. When it is all said and done, a good relationship with your teen is much more important than a clean bedroom! As you choose to focus on building a good relationship with them, what you think will have more of an impact on their lives because they will know you really care about them! Good news: it is never too late to shift your focus to them instead of their behavior. They will see this change in you, even if they don't want you to know they see it. The time will come, before you know it, that your child has left your home; then you can do whatever you want with that room.

Do you have a bedroom in which you're pretty sure there is a bed, but you just haven't seen it for a while? Better apply The System while you can still get in the door! Now make that room serve you as an office, craft or guest room.

Guest room

I have read several articles about "things your guests won't tell you." Here are some of my favorites:

- "My water glass left a ring mark on the bedside table." A table with a glass top will not do this. You can add a glass top to your existing table, or make sure a coaster is handy.

- "After turning out the lights, I bruised my knee climbing into bed!" Instead of depending on harsh overhead lighting, try a bedside table lamp. Not only does it cast a soft light, your guests won't have to navigate their way back to bed in an unfamiliar place. A nightlight might also be appreciated.

- "I'm hungry." Guests don't want to be caught in your fridge or pantry. Leaving a small bowl of snacks or fruit will curb their craving or offer a midnight snack.

- "Wow! That is a giant bouquet!" Bigger is not always better; a few buds will leave room on the bedside table for their essentials.

- "I can't find a place to charge my phone." Providing a power strip will keep your guests from crawling on all fours in search of an outlet!

It is useless for you to work so hard from early morning until late at night, anxiously working for food to eat; for God gives rest to his loved ones.
~ Psalm 127:2

Sleep matters

Delight and discovery were what I experienced at the Ana Crown Plaza Hotel while in Japan. Occasionally my sweet husband Len would ask me what I thought about "this" or "that" as he worked on our travel plans for the next few days.

Unfortunately, he did not have my full attention because I was entrenched in a "Sleep Advantage" brochure provided by the hotel. Determined to get my money's worth, I carefully followed each step in the brochure. It promised me that I would "sleep tight and welcome a lovely morning". The first thing I did was release a fragrant powder into the water as I drew a bath at precisely the correct temperature. I was amazed that the temperature was clearly marked on the actual faucet, making it easy to get it right! After my delightful bath I enjoyed slipping into the plush robe and slippers that the hotel had provided. Next I sipped a cup of low-caffeinated green tea as I waited for my "complimentary scent," which would be arriving soon from room service. An Italian hotel employee, the only one available who spoke some English, delivered my "scent." From his gestures, I was pretty sure that all I needed to do was place the little dish on the night stand to enjoy the aroma while sleeping. I then carefully set out the morning brew of green tea, which promised to energize me with just enough caffeine. I felt a little like Goldilocks as I followed the next step and tried to choose from the five different pillows that were amply supplied. Much to my delight I finally found the one that was "just right". Curiously I opened and applied the "eye warmer mask" that gently released heat, much like the ones we slip into our gloves in the winter! Snuggling under the covers, with eyes warming, and breathing in the sweet mandarin fragrance that was wafting in my direction, I asked my husband in a very relaxed voice to take my picture: I wanted to remember this — all of it!

I not only remembered this experience, I realized that sleep was important to this hotel and perhaps to this culture. Life is stressful, and it becomes even more stressful due to lack of sleep! Fatigue is one of the most common health complaints among women in our country. How many hours of shut-eye do you usually get? Is it enough? Some people can get by with less sleep than others need, and sometimes we have to, but we all need sleep for our physical and mental wellbeing. Research shows that those of us who get 6–8 hours of sleep a night are usually healthier and more productive than those who get less sleep. Rest is marked by a reduction of metabolic activity; it provides a chance for us to refresh our bodies and minds and to fill our energy levels back up.

Here are some sleep tips that hopefully will help you get the sleep you need.

Sleep tips:

- Caffeine can disrupt the ability to sleep. If you think you should avoid caffeine, don't have any caffeinated drinks after 2 p.m. Caffeine can stay in your system for an average of three to five hours, but some people are affected for as long as twelve hours. Caffeine is in most soft drinks, tea, and chocolate. Also be wary of certain medications, such as decongestants and certain antidepressants; they could be the cause of your sleep problems.

- Chamomile tea has been used for thousands of years to calm and soothe the muscular and nervous systems and to promote sleep, so it is a great bedtime brew. It is non-caffeinated and may help relax you for sleep.

- Choose your evening snack wisely! An oatmeal-raisin cookie and a glass of milk can help you fall asleep. That's because this snack includes complex carbohydrates that can increase levels of the sleep-inducing amino acid tryptophan. Other sleep-boosting choices: a piece of whole grain toast or a small bowl of cereal.

- Studies have also found that lavender produces relaxing and calming effects when inhaled. You can make or purchase little lavender pillows to place over your closed eyes or to keep near your regular pillow while sleeping. You can also make a lavender mist to spray on your pillow case just before bed time; there are many recipes online.

- Exercise in the day so you can sleep at night.

- Spend time right after dinner to plan your next day, look over your mail, or tie up loose ends so you don't have to think about those matters later when you are getting ready for bed.

- A few hours before bed, let your body know it is time to wind down by: turning off the computer, dimming the lights, taking a warm bath, reading a good book, or listening to some soothing music.

- To keep things calm: avoid scary movies, lively conversations, competitive games, or anything that will get you worked up or stressed out before bedtime.

- Avoid sleeping in.

- Get on a sleep schedule; start by getting to bed and getting up at the same time every day of the week, including weekends if you can.

- If you like to nap, keep the naps short and before 3 p.m. Whether you should nap during the day depends on how you normally sleep at night. If you typically sleep well, then an occasional short nap is OK. Naps can make you function better, lower your blood pressure, and maybe even help you live longer.

- Try to keep your bedrooms dark, cool, and quiet for the best sleep.

Creating your own personal retreat

What are the advantages of creating your own personal retreat? Imagine with me walking into a luxurious room in a very nice hotel. Can you see yourself enjoying a wonderful night's sleep or even taking a nap in that beautiful bed? Are you ready to kick your shoes off and move in? Now imagine again with me experiencing those same possibilities as you enter into your bedroom! You have already done the hard work of decluttering your bedroom. Perhaps you have even customized your room with some of the suggestions in this chapter. When you prioritize making your bedroom into a private retreat, you will be amazed how your quality of life will improve right along with your quality of sleep! You might need to shift your thinking about your bedroom, thinking "master retreat" instead of "catch-all." Once this shift is etched in your mind and becomes reality, you might even find yourself leaving your bedroom door open!

"Are you tired? Worn out? Burned out on religion? Come to me. Get away with me and you'll recover your life. I'll show you how to take a real rest. Walk with me and work with me — watch how I do it. Learn the unforced rhythms of grace. I won't lay anything heavy or ill-fitting on you. Keep company with me and you'll learn to live freely and lightly."
~ Matthew 11:28-30 (The Message)

Maintenance – Keep it tidy and organized!

Unfortunately, once you have decluttered your bedrooms and purposed them for rest, they won't automatically stay that way. You will need to make and enforce a declaration: do not bring anything into your bedroom that does not belong here! As you adjust to your new mindset, you will be keeping each of your bedrooms conducive to rest and relaxation. Now it's time to celebrate! You are reducing your stress level and winning the battle against clutter, one room at a time! Why not take a nap?!?

In this chapter

You learned the benefit of creating retreat-like bedrooms for the best sleep possible! I hope you discovered ways that will help you and family members make beds easily each morning – and enjoy it too! It's the little things that make a big difference, so pamper yourself with the suggestions in this chapter! While you're at it, place a small vase of flowers (picked from your yard along with a couple sprigs of greenery) on the bedside table; don't just reserve this nice touch for guests! Framing either (or both) of these scriptures will remind you that God's plan for us includes sleep and rest.

He lets me rest in green meadows; He leads me beside peaceful streams.
~ Psalm 23:2

Then Jesus said, "Come to me, all of you who are weary and carry heavy burdens, and I will give you rest."
~ Matthew 11:28

In the next chapter

Hold on to your hat because we are going to take purging to a new level! You will also see how to utilize the closet space you already have, which will save you time and money, once you can easily find what you need and already own. In your closet you will be able to dress faster because your closet is organized. And that's not all! You will learn to "shop" in your closet to create new outfits!

Chapter 6

———❦———

Closets
Do you really need more?

Scripture

*And regardless of what else you put on, wear love. It's your basic,
all-purpose garment. Never be without it.*
~ Colossians 3:14 (The Message)

In this chapter you will find help in:

- taking purging to a new level
- utilizing the closet space you already have
- saving time and money, when you can find what you need and already own
- dressing faster by organizing your closet
- shopping in your closet to create new outfits

Blast from the past:

From 1935 to 1959 a popular radio show aired called The Fibber McGee and Molly Show. The phrase "Fibber McGee's Closet" was coined from this show. In every episode the listener had to visualize the door of this over-stuffed hall closet as it opened, sending all its contents crashing to the floor! Perhaps that is not too hard to imagine. A closet can be a great resource where you can store and retrieve what you need — or it can be a place where you, like the McGees, need to post a sign: "Caution When Opening!"

A place for everything and everything in its place

This is not just a catchy saying; it is essential for keeping our homes tidy and organized, especially closets. Most of us have entertained the thought, If only I had more closets. I am convinced the solution is not more closets. It would probably not take us very long to fill them up, resulting in more to clean, organize and maintain. If you really are short on closets, help is on the way. But I warn you that there are some difficult decisions ahead of you. The exciting part is that, as you make them, you will see your closet-related stress melt away!

How many closets are we talking about?

Take a minute to think of all of the closets you have and which ones stress you the most. Is it your linen closet that barely stays tidy for a day? Perhaps your hall closet makes Fibber McGee's closet sound like nothing. Maybe your children's closets have become home to much more than their clothes. How about your clothes closet — is getting dressed a stressful ordeal?

On the move

In the following pages we will travel together to each of these closets where we will:
- determine the best use for each one
- discover practical fun ways to reclaim space
- store what you have, making it easier to find what you need

Think before you buy

I used to get so excited about a new purchase just because it was a bargain. I love getting a good deal on something (I still do), but I often had buyer's remorse when I realized that I really did not need it, had no place to put it, or that someone had the same thing that I could easily borrow on occasion. Now, many times I have left the store without purchasing something I wanted. After a few days, if I am still thinking about that particular item, I reconsider the purchase. A few times I have returned to the store to find that the item I wanted is no longer available; I usually recover! I try to make a "chance" purchase only if I can return it to the store. I like to ask at the time of purchase if the item can be returned with cash back, then I know their policy. Store credit is only good if I shop there regularly; when I don't, it is easy to forget I have the credit and never use it. If you are tempted to make purchases that you might regret, consider writing yourself a little note and placing it in the money or credit card compartment of your wallet to remind you to "think before you buy"!

Ready to start?

How often a closet is used (and by whom) will determine the effort needed to declutter, organize and keep it maintained. I encourage you to work on one closet at a time. You decide if you want to tackle the most stressful one first or last; there are advantages to both. If you rated closets high on your stress evaluation (Chapter 1), you might want to work on your most challenging closet last. Being able to look at and enjoy the ones you have already organized will fuel you with satisfaction and the energy to finish your closets right down to that last one! If time is a factor for you, tackling your most challenging closet first will reduce your stress as quickly as possible! Either way, apply The System (Chapter 1) to each closet before organizing. If you lack courage, read the section of that chapter again, and then do what you need to do! It is imperative that you become ruthless in your purging during the "throw away" and "give away" steps. Keep in mind that what you do not get rid of has to go somewhere! Remember: after you have successfully accomplished applying The System, you will have less to put away!

Linen Closets can be found in hallways, bathrooms or bedrooms.

- Where do you store your linens? Do you need to store other items in there too?
- What items can you group together, like: towels, sheets, blankets, seldom used items?
- Can you store each group on a shelf — or on half of a shelf? Can you label each shelf?
- Consider storing some of your items in baskets that you can label. (Note: Labeling will help family members return items to where they belong.)
- Top shelf: place blankets or items you seldom use, like sleeping bags, humidifier, etc.
- Designate a shelf / half-shelf (depending on space) for each of the following items: sheets, towels, guest room items, miscellaneous.

Towels and Sheets: Keep your closet neater longer by rolling your sheets and bath towels. For towels: fold in half width-wise, fold again, and then roll. You can either roll or fold hand towels. I fold mine the way they hang on the towel bar so I can grab and hang them quickly. I place them in front of the rolled bath towels. Wash cloths can be rolled too or folded in squares and placed in front of the rolled towels. I have a large basket under my sink in open-shelving in which I store the rolled wash cloths I use every day. They are easily reached, saving me from dripping over to my linen closet for a cloth. If you have special towels for guests, you could store them at the back of your towel shelf, or on a separate shelf, or in a guest room closet (you can find more guest room ideas in the bedroom chapter). If you have several bathrooms, you might want to color coordinate your towels so you will easily know where each goes after laundering. If you have more towels than closet space, roll them and then place in a large basket located close to your tub or shower.

Surprise!

When my kids started changing their own sheets, I soon discovered that they were only changing the top sheet, which explained how they got it done so fast! This is when I started rolling the fitted and top sheet along with the pillowcase together in a pack. This not only solved my problem, it also made it easier for them to find their sheets and kept the linen closet neat too!

I like to roll sheets too. For sheets: tuck fitted ends together at ends, holding lengthwise and folding over. Do the same with the flat sheet. Lay the fitted sheet on top of the flat and place the pillowcase(s) on top. Now gently roll together, creating a pack. The beauty behind the rolling is that, as you pull out what you need, the other towels and sheets will stay neatly in place, even if you pull from the middle.

Hall closet

If you have one, what do you use it for—coats, games, anything and everything?

Coats: Only store the current season and you will have more space. If you would like to use this closet for guests coats, store your coats on a coat tree placed by the door you use the most. (Guests can always place their coats on a bed if you have a crowd or no closet space to offer.) Other items that could be stored in a hall closet are hats, gloves, umbrellas, etc. You can store these items in an over-the-door-type storage unit, designating a few pockets for each family member or type of item.

Games, puzzles, etc.: As mentioned in the media chapter (Chapter 4), these can be place on a shelf if you have the space. If you don't have much space, consider removing games and puzzles from their boxes and placing each one in a sturdy plastic zippered bag. (You can put the tape away because you will no longer have to keep repairing those ripped boxes!) I cut the name of the game/puzzle off each box and store it, along with any instructions or photos, in the bag with each game. Retrieval of any game is easy when you can see the name, and keeping the picture is essential for puzzles, unless your skills are extraordinaire! You can store pencils, paper, timer, cards, dice, etc., in another bag for use with several different games. Now you can store all of your games and puzzles neatly in a basket on a closet shelf — or on the floor if you need to.

Kids Closets are usually a challenge! With growing children you will have clothes they have grown out of and clothes they will grow into. Clear bins placed on a top shelf are a good way to store this type of clothing. If you have infants, I encourage you to hang the next size of clothing so you will see them. My first child did not get to wear several cute outfits because I did not try them on him in time — I did not make that mistake again! We were blessed with clothing from friends and family with older children; you might consider passing on what you no longer need. Choosing clothes the night before or arranging clothing in outfits can save you time and energy in the morning. If your children can't reach to hang their clothes up, consider providing a stool or hanging a lower rod.

Bitter Sweet: I remember when my kids were learning to put their freshly laundered clothes away. I watched with parental pride as they each collected their clothes and marched to their rooms to put the clothes away. Sweet turned bitter when I saw those clothes shoved into drawers or left sitting in the bottom of their closets! It took some time for me to understand that their definition of "putting their clothes away" was different from mine. There is such a fine line between training children to become responsible for their own things and not discouraging them with standards that are too high.

✑*Don't give up!*

It is at this point that many parents think it is just easier to do the job themselves. Many do, and they are right; it is easier! Training children is never easy, but if we don't train them we have robbed them of that feeling of accomplishment and of learning to take responsibility. These are basic "life skills." Just one more thought for you parents: to keep this from being a constant battle, set some reasonable consequences for not doing what is asked or expected, like no TV, video games, etc., if their clothes are not put away. Now you have placed the ball in their court. They are responsible for what they get to do, making it their choice. There is no need for you to nag or get mad; you can even commiserate with them by agreeing that you wish they had chosen to do their job so they could play, but rules are rules! Kids are smart, and they will soon learn what they have to do to get to do what they want!

Less is best! When applying The System to your children's closets, remember: less is best! The less they have, the easier it will be for them to manage. If your children are old enough to help with this process, you will be teaching how to declutter. Try sectioning off areas in drawers for underwear, socks, pajamas, etc. This will help corral like items together. For small clothes, a shoe box lid will work; use a larger lid, box or a bin for larger sized clothes. The children can still toss their clothing into a drawer — but in a designated spot.

Chaos to Calm: If you have a designated play room, I encourage you to keep toys out of small children's bedrooms. This will make nap-time easier as they won't be tempted to get up and play when you are not looking. If your kids toys need to stay in their rooms, try to confine them to a specific area (like a play corner) or in the closet. You can section off an area with a bookshelf and a bean bag chair for reading. In their closets, use colored bins or boxes to store toys. Decorating and labeling each box will make clean-up fun and easy when they know where to put each type of toy. Label each box or bin with a picture for preschool children, and replace the picture with words as they begin to read.

Office: If your office is in a bedroom, you will have a closet in there. An upright file cabinet will slide under a pole bar nicely and will leave more room for office furniture (and a bed, if your office doubles as a guest room). If you are able to designate this space mostly for office items, consider installing more shelves. You will find more ideas in the office chapter (Chapter 7).

Miscellaneous ideas

If you have extra closets or some extra space in a closet, why not consider:

- Sewing bin, where you store everything you need for mending.
- Gift box or shelf, where you create your own store, containing gift items for your friends, children, etc. Buy items that are on sale, and then shop from your box or shelf, eliminating last-minute, expensive and stressful gift buying! I implemented this when my kids had more birthday parties than I had money or patience.
- Gift wrapping shelf, basket or area, where your supplies are conveniently stored together so you can get the job done quickly.

Your Clothes Closet

For most of us this is the most frustrating closet, because we personally deal with it every day! Imagine with me a pleasant place where you can easily select any piece of clothing you want to wear because everything is ready to wear and is an option for you. No more trying on three or four outfits until you find something suitable. Seem too good to be true? It's not — if you are willing to be brutally honest with yourself as you apply The System to your closet and only replace the clothing that you will wear and that is ready to wear!

Let's walk through The System together for this one!

Throw away things that have found their way into your closet that need to be trashed! (One class participant found a few boxes of cookies she had hidden from her kids that were now stale!) Clothing that is not good enough to pass on could become rags.

Give away clothing that you no longer need or use. Make sure it is still in good condition. Share these with family and friends, or find another venue that takes gently used clothes.

Not Sure: These are clothes you think you might wear again or really like but never wear. Hang these on a different type or color of hanger so they are easily identified. Over the next month, force yourself to wear them; if you can't bring yourself to wear them, get rid of them now!

Put away any items that are not clothes—try not to store non-clothing items in your closet unless you have absolutely nowhere else to store them. Box and mark those items clearly so you know what they are, and place them on a high shelf.

Designate an area for clothes that need to be repaired or ironed as you are applying the "put away" step of the system. I hang this category of clothing for two reasons: so I can see them, reminding me that they need my attention, and because hanging prevents more wrinkles from setting in. Most of the clothing I buy does not need to be ironed, but some need the collar, cuffs or the facing (where the buttons and buttons holes are) pressed. I do have to hang these items that are my husband's where he cannot see them—to prevent embarrassment (mine)!

Declare a moratorium on all clothes-buying until your closet is completely decluttered and organized! This may motivate you to get the job done faster and will prevent you from adding to your mess.

Discard: If your budget allows, replace any wire hangers. You can purchase slim hangers that take up less closet space, plastic hangers work quite well. I like to use all the same color, and I have found that baby hangers work great for camisoles and some of my sleeveless tops.

Funny story

Our youngest son discovered a box of good clothes sitting on a neighbor's garbage can. Excited about his discovery, he was sure I would dash right over there to retrieve the box. I was excited too but chose to wait until it was dark to grab the treasure. The box contained several cute outfits for children. I ended up giving most of it away because the sizes were too small for my kids, but I did find a dress for my daughter. She wore it to school the very next day! Returning home from kindergarten, my daughter told me that her teacher liked her dress. My smile quickly turned to an expression of shock: she had also told her teacher that her mom found the dress in the garbage! Humbled and embarrassed would describe how I felt as I walked into my parent-teacher meeting that week.

Display: Arranging your clothing by color and type will help you:
- find clothes easily
- combine clothes to make new outfits
- know what you have too many of (like white shirts)
- know what you may need to buy
- keep your closet looking great

This is fairly easy to do. Replace your clothes in sections: hang all of your pants together, skirts together, dresses together, jackets together and tops together. Now arrange each group by color, going from light to dark. Arrange each color of tops by sleeve length, from sleeveless to long-sleeve. If you have double hanging rods in your closet, hang pants and jackets on the lower pole and tops on the top. You will now be able to find and replace clothing in your closet quickly.

I found a great application for my phone: I take a photo of each clothing item, placing them then in categories. The cool thing is: I can make outfits with my own clothes. If this interests you, check out some style applications. I am also reminded what clothes I already have!

I took a photo with my phone of my closet that is arranged this way to remind me not to buy clothing in white or brown and to add brighter colors. Another trick I learned is to hang the clothes you have just worn or laundered in the opposite direction in your closet. After a period of time you will see what you are wearing and, more important, what you are not. When I did this, I forced myself to choose from the clothes I had not worn. The items I did not wear were given away, freeing up space for what I did wear. I do this periodically to keep my closet cleaned out. Once I discovered a jacket that I had not worn for a long time. I hung it on the door knob, giving it one last chance, determined to wear it that week or out it would go. When I wore it, my friend complimented me on it and said if I ever wanted to get rid of it, to send it her way. This was going to be a win-win situation whatever my final decision was.

Poor to rich

We women are accused of saying "I have nothing to wear" when we have a closet full of clothes! Perhaps you men say that too. I confess that I have said it and felt this way too many times. A statistic I actually believe is that most of us wear 20% of our clothes 80% of the time! When our closets house a variety of styles and sizes we no longer wear, it becomes necessary to reach for what we feel comfortable in, know looks good, or really like. Clear out your closet, and you will be amazed at the treasures you will find hiding in there! You are rich indeed — when you can wear everything in your closet!

Shop your closet

Most of us really do have something in our closet that we could wear for an upcoming Christmas party or special occasion. Designate some time and "shop your closet," trying on clothes with jackets, belts, scarves, jewelry and shoes. After you have put together a few outfits, you will want to remember them, especially if you are not accustomed to wearing those items together. Carefully lay the outfit out on the bed and take a photo, or have someone take a photo of you with it on. Store your photos in a "go to" folder.

A friend creates outfits from her closet for the Christmas season and then hangs everything, right down to the necklace, on a hanger. If you try her idea, you'll always look festive and have the satisfaction of wearing the seasonal items you already have. Best of all, it's like money in the bank knowing you have outfits you can wear for those parties that are coming up!

Another holiday idea is to twist a festive ribbon on the hangers of clothes that you could wear. They are easy to spot, like red or green clothing for Christmas, etc. After the occasion, just remove the ribbon.

Making time for this kind of "shopping" will save you time because you can eliminate those last minute, stressful shopping trips. Pressure shopping leaves me frustrated with the money I spent—and what I ended up with. Sometimes you do need to purchase something to complete an outfit or give it a new look. It is easy to know what you need when you can clearly see everything you have in your closet. Maybe an accessory is all you need to purchase to add to and to complete an outfit. Maybe a colorful jacket to go over a simple black dress will work. I also enjoy shopping my closet when I feel like I have nothing to wear, or when time or money is in short supply.

Make a list of the items you would like to add to your closet or need to complete an outfit. A list will also keep you from impulse buying.

Maintenance – Keep it tidy and organized!

Unfortunately, once your closets have been cleaned out and organized, they will not automatically stay that way. But they will be easier to periodically clean because you have moved out what does not belong in there and established a place for everything. I can put away freshly laundered clothes quite quickly because I have done this. I have to confess that I often like to toss my socks into their drawer and when they "somehow" are all jumbled together again, it just takes me a few minutes to straighten that drawer out! Not letting everything become completely chaotic again works out better for me. A little chaos is good for me—and my former perfectionist ways! It is important to discover what works best for you in keeping *Your Home Matters* stress low.

In this chapter

You identified all of the closets you have, and hopefully you will discover that after purging and decluttering, you have enough of them! I trust that some excitement has been generated as you read the tips and benefits of tackling your clothes closet! It feels good to wear all of your clothing and it feels great to create new outfits from what you already have.

> *And regardless of what else you put on, wear love. It's your basic,*
> *all-purpose garment. Never be without it.*
> ~ Colossians 3:14 (The Message)

In the next chapter

You will learn ways to use your current office space, as well as re-purpose items for office use. How about developing a personalized filing system that will work for you? Imagine finding what you need quickly, and eliminating all of those stacks of paper! Let's do it together!

Chapter 7

———

Office Area
Finding what you need when you need it

Scripture

*For God did not give us a spirit of fear and timidity,
but of power, love, and self-discipline.*
~ 2 Timothy 1:7

True confession: Just mentioning the word "office" can make my blood run cold (this scripture verse needs to be on my desk)! This is the most challenging area of my home, probably because I am the one responsible for our household and business bookkeeping. The office area rated very high on the stress evaluation for class participants too. It is amazing the amount of paper we have to deal with on a daily basis: bills that need to be paid, information that needs to be filed, junk that just needs to be thrown away! I am excited to say that I am continuing to learn effective ways to run my office in a satisfying and efficient way while reducing my stress, and I hope that will be the same for you.

In this chapter you will find help in:
- utilizing your current office space
- repurposing items for office use
- developing a personalized system that will work for you
- eliminating stacks of papers
- finding what you need quickly
- going green — reducing paper where you can

We are going to separate the work in your office into two categories, first the space where you work, and then working in your space! Your office space may be a designated room, an alcove or even a closet! You may have several areas that are used for office space by family members, or perhaps you share an office.

Your Office Space
Ready to start?

Throw away

As you apply The System (Chapter 1) to each of the areas that are described as office space, be ruthless in throwing anything out that hinders production. Much like the laundry room, your office can quickly become a dropping-off place for items that do not belong there. This is not the best place for storage, unless you have the room or no other option. During the "throw away" step, dispose of the obvious. Remember: we will get to the paperwork later, so resist the temptation to start going through those papers now. If you have paperwork stored in boxes, stack them in a closet or a corner of the room for now.

Give away

Do you have a stack of magazines as tall as a toddler? I remember having a huge stack of magazines I wanted to go through for recipes, decorating, craft ideas and the like. The problem was, I never seemed to take the time to go through them. My pile grew as I moved it from area to area. Those treasures finally ended up in my bedroom. I thought I would go through a few each night, but I didn't, and I ended up shoving them under my bed because I was tired of looking at them! Months later, trying to vacuum around them again, I did something I never thought I could do: I marched them out to the trash can, and in they went—after only a slight hesitation. It felt so good to toss them! But if you absolutely cannot toss, recycle. (I wish I had thought of that, but I am still so glad that they are gone!) You could give them away to friends—warning: choose your recipients wisely, so that you aren't adding to their clutter. Another option would be to donate current issues to a local doctor's or dentist's office for the waiting room. If you have more magazines coming than you can read, consider subscribing online or canceling some of your sub-scriptions; that is what I have done.

More giveaway ideas:

- Go through your books and remove the ones you no longer need or want. You might consider selling school books or requested titles to online companies that buy used books.
- Recycle or find a home for dated, faded, wrinkled and crinkled paper.

Put away

Are projects taking up your office space? Find another area for these too. Store everything that you need for the project in an appro-priately sized basket that can travel to a work area, like your dining room or kitchen table. When you are finished for the day, toss every-thing back in the basket. Baskets help you keep everything together in one place. This simple step eliminates clutter build-up and keeps these areas serviceable for what they were intended for, like dining, and keeps your supplies from walking away. Resist thinking, Why put this away? I will be working on this again tomorrow. You may or you may not get to it for a while! You can store baskets on the top shelf of closets.

If you have several projects, store your supplies in stacking boxes or baskets for a neater appearance. Hang a label from each one for easy recognition. Using this system allows you to work on a project easily, since you won't have to "round up" your supplies every time.

Other features of your office space:

- If you need a desk in your office area, you have more options than a conventional one. You can use any flat surface, like a table or even an old door! Creating an L-shaped working space is convenient when you need a place for a computer, printer, etc., and also space to spread out. There are some great ideas on the internet to get your creative juices flowing.

- Try to find a comfortable chair that is adjustable; wheels are helpful, especially for working in an L-shaped space. Wheels are not good if your office has carpet, unless you place your chair on a large (enough to reach) office mat. Another idea is to place a low nap rug (enabling your chair to move) over your carpet.

- During many of our moves that required a temporary living situation, I did not have the luxury of filing cabinets. I have even had to store file boxes under the table I used for a desk. My preference is to use hanging files on a frame with wheels that easily slide under a table/desk. Covering this table with a black twin flat sheet works great, it hangs down far enough to conceal what is stored underneath, and the color stays clean.

- Bookcases or shelving units work great in an office area. To keep them looking neat, stack supplies or place them in baskets before putting them on shelves. You can attach baskets on the end of your bookcase for more storage and even designate one for each family member.

- Give consideration to good lighting. Cleaning your light fixture will make a huge improvement, so will replacing the bulb to a higher wattage (maximum wattage is usually indicated on the fixture).

Keeping it tidy

Landscape the top of your desk with just the items you use regularly to free up work space. Store other items in a drawer or basket.

While you are scouting out possible items to use in an office area, be on the lookout for two baskets or two decorative boxes that you can use for your incoming and outgoing paperwork/mail. Chances are you already own something that would work great. This is an efficient way to control paper and be able to find what you need. I have no idea how much time I have wasted looking for a particular piece of mail or paperwork; having a specific place to toss it solves that problem!

If you have an abundance of pens, have a child help to "test" each one, tossing the ones that do not work.

Find a new place for items that are in your way. You can use small boxes, tuna cans or small containers for items like rubber bands, paper clips, etc.; group them in your drawer much like the section dividers you can buy. For a nice touch, spray paint them when you have the time.

Storing your surplus supply of paper, pens, pencils, etc., somewhere other than in your desk will keep your desk drawers from getting jam-packed.

Extra step

Consider redecorating office space to reflect the interests of the person using it. Hanging pictures and memorabilia will make the time spent in there more enjoyable. If you like to travel, hang a map indicating the places you have been or would like to travel to. Frame your licenses and certificates in interesting frames or make a collage out of them.

Your paperwork

What the world really needs is more love and less paperwork!
~ Pearl Bailey

Ready to start?

The System will work a little differently when applied to your paperwork.

Throw away

Locate a large trash can — you're probably going to need it! You will also need to do some shredding during the "throw away" step of the system. It is not necessary to shred the entire document, just the area that has your personal identification information on it, like name, address, account number, social security number, etc. You do not need to go out and purchase a shredder; perhaps you can borrow one or shred the old-fashioned way, with your hands, tearing several sheets at the same time. I use the old-fashioned way more than I use my shredder; it's fast and easy, and I always know where it is! Another option is to safely burn personal documents.

Throw away any paperwork that you no longer need or that you have stored or backed up electronically.

Some paperwork you need to keep

How long do I keep this?
- ATM receipts – 1 month until statement confirms transaction
- Bank statements – 1 year; annual statement – 7 yrs.
- Credit card statements – 1 year; annual statement – 7 yrs.
- Long term mortgage statements – 1 year; annual statement – 7 yrs.
- Medical bills – until paid off; final proof of payment – 1 yr.
- Tax documents – 7 yrs.
- Home improvement receipts – until you sell the home
- Investment documents – indefinitely

Keep forever

- Family birth and death certificates, baptism and confirmation certificates, marriage certificates, divorce decrees, adoption papers, military service records and discharge papers
- Legal documents (store these in a personal safe or a safety deposit box)
- Wills and medical directives, social security cards, citizenship/ naturalization records, licenses to practice your profession, trust or power of attorney, contracts, titles of vehicles

Keep at home

- Passports (make a copy to take with you and one copy to leave home when traveling), legal cases paper work and contracts (divorce and work), jury duty recognition of service
- Auto information: Car title and bill of sale, insurance policy
- Property information: home deed, title insurance policy, property insurance policy (If you have a mortgage, your lender has your note.)
- Burial and plot deeds
- Insurance and investments: stock certificates, life insurance policy paperwork, pension and retirement benefit agreements
- Pay statements (There is no need to save pay stubs, but do save the annual statements in case you need to show proof of employment.)

I hate junk mail!

Go online to find the current procedure to "opt out" of receiving junk mail. This is something that you may have to do periodically, but it is worth it. You can also find out how to keep your phone numbers (both home and cell) from being called by solicitors.

Give away

Designate some file folders or expandable files for information you want to give to someone.

Put away only what you need!

You will need to round up some file folders or hanging files, labels and a pencil. There is no need to purchase new file folders if you have some you can use; it is quite easy to replace them once all the sorting and filing has been done.

Step by step:

- As you go through your papers, make temporary piles by category on your desk or floor.

- Write on the file folder or label the categories represented by your piles to file.

- Transfer each pile of paperwork into a file folder. Use hanging files if a regular folder is too small.

- It is not necessary to sort through these now. Having corralled them into file folders by category is a huge step! You can designate a chunk of time to go through the files or go through them a file at a time as you can. You can also do this if you have boxes of paperwork that you need to go through.

- I suggest using hanging files for larger categories with several smaller files inside.

- If you have several insurance policies, etc., you might consider creating a three-ring binder with dividers. Color-code each policy, etc. Make an index sheet in the front of the binder reflecting the color of each policy and its expiration date. (Our agent actually did this for us, and I use it all the time.) Typical file categories: Banking – Insurance – Utilities – Credit – Loans – Bills – Accounts – On line/Magazines – Correspondence – Directories/addresses

- Transfer your files to a filing cabinet, portable file system, or a file-size box that can be purchased at an office supply store.

- Position your file labels either all on the right or left side. They are much easier to read this way.

Keeping it tidy and organized!

This is one of the most challenging areas of a home to keep efficient and free of clutter. Weekly cleaning and application of The System, when you are not in the middle of a project like taxes, will keep this area running like a fine-tuned machine. This is so much easier than letting it all go and having to find the desk again!

Bills:

- I use a wooden napkin holder my daughter made for us when she was in grade school to hold bills I need to pay.

- You can use an expandable file-type system to keep current with your bills. Label each section by category and place bills to be paid in there, or you can make monthly labels.

- For online bills, I jot down the payee, amount and due date in a sectioned spiral notebook I keep by my computer. In the business section I draw columns; in the bill column I make a notation when I have paid a bill online so I know that I still have to enter it into my bookkeeping software. Once that is done, I make a notation that it has been paid. (I do not delete the e-bill until I have paid the bill and recorded it.) I have another column for calls to make, necessary correspondence to complete, items to purchase, and things to look up on the internet, etc. I have found that it is less likely I will lose my notebook than scraps of paper with information on them. This system is not foolproof, but the more I use it, the more I realize that it does work.

- Create either a 3 x 5 or 4 x 6 file card for each utility company you have an account with. Mark the name, contact information, and your account number on the card. On the back write in pencil who you talked to and the date you talked to that person when you make changes to your account. This is helpful if you have to call the company again. Now you can keep track of your promotional discounts, etc. (I call my phone and cable company periodically to see if they can lower my bill, and much to my delight they usually can.)

Maintenance – Keep it tidy and organized!

Most office organizational systems forbid storing anything horizontally. It is impossible to file every paper immediately after reading it! Use your incoming receptacle, and go through it weekly. Likewise, when you have deposits ready to be banked, papers for a meeting, and paperwork for your friend or mail that needs posting, place these in your outgoing receptacle. Now you just have to grab what you need on your way to the door. Experiment to see what works best for you.

In this chapter

You discovered that keeping areas you use for an office free of clutter is not an easy job – but one that is well worth it. Especially when you can find what you need when you need it! Organizing your office space with receptacles you already have keeps the process moving forward and saves you money too! Remember our powerful scripture verse for this chapter whenever you feel weak in the knees!

For God did not give us a spirit of fear and timidity, but of power,
love, and self-discipline.
~ 2 Timothy 1:7

In the next chapter

We will arrange your kitchen for ease in meal preparation and cooking as well as finding the best use for the area you have. I hope you are ready to work faster and enjoy your time in the kitchen too. I think you will enjoy the stories! Who knows? You may soon be ready to appear on one of those cooking shows!

Chapter 8

Kitchen
Where everyone ends up...

Scripture

Offer hospitality to one another without grumbling.
~ 1 Peter 4:9 (NIV)

In this chapter you will find help in:
- arranging your kitchen for ease in meal preparation and cooking
- finding the best use for the area you have
- working faster and enjoying it

No matter where I serve my guests,
they seem to like my kitchen best!

Grand Central Station could be another name for this area of your home! Sooner or later everybody seems to end up in the kitchen. If yours is a disaster, help is on the way! There are several things you can do to make your kitchen more efficient. As you apply The System to this area, you will be well on your way to creating a space that is more useful and fun to be in.

Be encouraged by this story from Tonya, a *Your Home Matters* class participant...

"There was always excitement when Tonya brought refreshments to class. She was an excellent cook and even sold some of her specialty items. Because she used her kitchen extensively, plans to remodel it were in the making. Tonya shared with the class that after applying The System to her kitchen and rearranging it to be more efficient, remodeling was no longer necessary!"

Wow! A new kitchen without spending all that money! Stories like this are so encouraging, they motivate us to work with and make the best of what we already have — and in this case saving the family a substantial amount of money!

I have divided the kitchen into two chapters. The first one will cover the actual kitchen area of your home. The second chapter will be devoted to food inventory, food storage, grocery shopping and meals.

Ready to start?

Use The System (Chapter 1) on all of your cupboards, drawers and counter tops. Remember to throw away/recycle and give away, and then put away only what you really need. Is it really necessary to have two vegetable peelers (etc.) in your drawer? Probably not, unless you have a helper and you plan on peeling together! You might consider making up a box of duplicate kitchen items to give away to someone who is setting up a first home, or a college student, or to take along on your next camping trip. You must be ruthless to gain the upper hand and win the battle against clutter — especially here!

After you have completed this step, you will only need to put away or rearrange what you really need, want and are currently using. By storing your most-used cooking utensils in a crock on your counter-top you can free up drawer space. If your kitchen storage is limited, you can store seldom-used items and small appliances in the garage or storage area. Be sure to clearly mark the boxes, so you can easily find these items again.

Zones

Divide your kitchen into two zones: cooking and baking. The cooking zone works best near your stove; this is where you place the items you use mostly for cooking. In the same way create a zone for items related to baking. The location of this zone should be close to your best counter space. If counter space is limited, choose a cupboard near your table, where you can spread out when baking. Because it is fairly easy to carry whatever you are going to bake to the oven, this zone does not have to be next to it.

Arrangement: Here are some specific ideas for placement of common kitchen items, for convenience:

- Dishes, glasses and silverware stored close to the dishwasher make unloading quicker. I prefer this instead of storing them close to the table. It is easier to carry dinnerware to the table than to carry clean dishes to a cabinet or hutch.
- Store coffee mugs near your coffee maker if you can.
- Conveniently keep all you need for an espresso, including the coffee, close to your machine and you will probably use it more.
- Place pots and pans near the stove where you use them — cooking zone.
- Baking items (pans, measuring utensils, etc.) kept together make baking easier — baking zone.
- Keep the cooking spices you use the most, sea salt, and olive oil by the stove.
- Separate your baking spices, and keep them together in a cupboard in the baking zone or in a removable container in your pantry.
- Alphabetize your spices; this might sound a little over the top, but I think you will like how easily you will be able to find them.
- Place items you seldom use in hard-to-reach cabinets, like over the fridge.
- A hutch, server, china cabinet, or even a dresser is a great place to store oversized serving dishes, placemats, and cloth napkins. If you store cloth napkins with scented candles, they will smell good; a fragrance sachet will also do the trick.
- Cleaning items are usually stored under the sink. Use child locks if there are small children in your home. By lining the bottom of this cupboard with water-repellent shelf paper, you will preserve the wood if any of your cleaners drip or spill.

More tips:

- Placing your dishes in groups in your dishwasher will cut your unloading time in half; place plates by size and type of silverware in one section of holder. Now you can grab several in one handful as you unload.

- For more counter space, store your small appliances in cupboards.

- If you keep your toaster in a cupboard, leave it in a sturdy plastic lid (shoe box size) or a durable tray that meat comes in. This will keep the crumbs contained, and not all over your counter; dump and wipe out when necessary.

- Store the cheaper kind of paper plates and a plate cover near your microwave. Ask family members to use them! If you do this, your microwave clean up time will consist of wiping it out, instead of scrubbing off baked-on food.

- Look to see if there is a perforated tab on your rolls of foil, plastic wrap and wax paper; punch them in to secure the roll, and your life will never be the same!

- If you roll your kitchen towels, they will fit and stay more neatly in a drawer.

- Use a paper towel roll to store your extension cord in, keeping it contained and tangle-free.

Recipe books can be stored in a cupboard, if you have the room. I have been working on storing mine on the computer. If this interests you, you can use a word- processing program or specific recipe software. I use a program that comes with Microsoft Office, called "One Note." My laptop sits on the counter when I am cooking, so I can view the recipe. I can easily make adjustments to the recipe too. Once recipes are electronically stored, sharing is easy, by email or printing. This project took quite a while to complete, but it was one I enjoyed working on in the evenings. If you decide to do this, give yourself time and enjoy it. Caution: it might make you hungry!

Before we leave the kitchen I want to share a few thoughts that help me keep the right perspective in offering hospitality.

HOSPITALITY	ENTERTAINING
Provides a safe place	Opens a show place
Seeks to serve others	Wants to impress others
Places people before things	Elevates things above people
Makes what is mine yours	Claims all as mine and admires it
Takes no thought for whatever reward	Expects praise and reciprocation
	Models itself after the world
Frames itself according to God's Word	Becomes a taskmaster, requiring you to meet the expectations of others
Offers freedom that liberates, enabling you to exercise your gifts and creativity to the fullest	

Adapted from Thomas Nelson, The Woman's Study Bible

Making hospitality easier:

- If you are comfortable and at ease, your guests will feel comfortable and at ease too!

- The most appreciated area to clean is the bathroom guests will be using. Check out the bathroom chapter (Chapter 11) to learn how to clean one in ten minutes!

- Prepare something easy to eat, preferably something you have made before.

- Pray for your guests during your preparation for their visit. When I remember to do this, I feel excited about our time together and connected with them before they arrive.

- I mop the floors after people leave, especially if we are having a lot of people in our home. I usually vacuum or spot clean any sticky floor area. If I mop, I'll just have to do it again when everyone is gone — and that is a waste of energy!

- Think about something you would enjoy doing with your guests after dinner. It is nice to move to another area for dessert and coffee — having what you need, like cups, plates, utensils, cream and sugar, on a tray ahead of time makes this really easy. Perhaps your guests would enjoy playing a fun card game with you. Time spent visiting with new friends or catching up with friends you already know is always fun. Asking each person a few questions during the course of conversation will give everyone a chance to talk.

I still prefer "inviting" guests to our home, but I have found some ways to enjoy those impromptu visits too.

- When I receive my unexpected guests just as they are, they receive me just as I am too!
- So what if they have to step over laundry as they come in the back door? They too have dirty laundry that needs to be washed!
- Sometimes we have areas in our homes that are a "work in progress"; guests are usually interested in what you are doing or planning to do — relax and let them in on your plans.
- If you have guests who drop in on a regular basis, you might want to keep on hand what you need to make a few easy meals — or have your favorite pizza place on speed dial.

> *Better a dry crust eaten in peace than a house*
> *filled with feasting – and conflict.*
> ~ Proverbs 17:1

I love this verse: it reminds me that I can generate peace to those in my home and that I probably have more than a dry crust of bread to offer them.

Maintenance – Keep it tidy and organized!

You will need to make some strategic plans to keep your kitchen counters from becoming a "catch all" again. Use a basket, decorative dish, or even a flower pot to create a place for whatever continues to end up on your counters. Now you have a place to toss mail, school papers, coupons, etc. To manage this place, plan to go through it periodically, tossing everything you can in the trash, and putting the rest away. If you have a surplus of drawers in your kitchen, consider using one for miscellaneous items. (This is also known as the "junk drawer.") Use small boxes or a silverware divider to section the contents. This will prevent useful items from getting lost in there.

In this chapter

You learned about some simple and efficient ways to make your kitchen better. Get ready to save yourself some time and money as you apply these tips. I hope that you will consider inviting some friends into your home; if you keep it simple you are more apt to make this a fun habit.

> *Offer hospitality to one another without grumbling.*
> ~ 1 Peter 4:9 (NIV)

In the next chapter

I will show you how creating an inventory of your pantry, refrigerator and freezer will help you avoid buying duplicates or wasting food. This strategy will also help you in simple meal planning and smart shopping. You are going to be amazed at what you can do!

Chapter 9

―――――❦―――――

Food Inventory, Meal Planning and Shopping
Life would be easier if we didn't have to eat!

Scripture

People do not live by bread alone,
but by every word that comes from the mouth of God.
~ Matthew 4:4

In this chapter you will find help in:
- creating an inventory of your pantry, refrigerator and freezer
- avoiding buying duplicates or wasting food
- simple meal planning
- smart shopping, saving you time and $$

It's a big responsibility feeding a family. Have you ever wondered how many meals you prepare in one year? (Maybe you don't really want to know!) My mom went to work when I was a teen, so I became responsible for some of the grocery shopping and meal making. Because of this experience, I thought I was a pretty good cook. Unfortunately, I had a false impression of my culinary skills. I cooked for my dad, and he seemed to love everything I made. One night I had prepared sweet and sour meatballs, and looking at my dad's expression, I realized that something was not quite right. Not wanting to discourage me, he managed to hoarsely say, in between coughing spasms, "Let's just let these sit for a while. I am sure they will taste great tomorrow when some of the vinegar has had a chance to evaporate… But this rice is sure good," he added in his hoarse voice.

After I married, keeping my husband fed was a big concern for me. Growing up on a farm made him a meat-and-potatoes kind of guy, and a hungry one at that. Before eating out or going to a friend's home, I tried to curb his appetite with a sandwich or two. With his appetite and my biased cooking reviews from my sweet dad, we both needed to make some adjustments. Fortunately for this teen bride and still-growing husband, several women at our church took me under their wings. They taught me cooking basics — and did not laugh at my questions like, "How do you fold flour into the batter?" Much to my surprise and my husband's delight, I even learned how to bake bread!

The Little Red Hen

I have to admit there have been many times when I felt like the "Little Red Hen." Do you remember the classic children's story, and the hen's dilemma? She could not find anyone to help her grow the grain, grind the wheat, or make and bake the bread — but everyone showed up when it was time to eat the bread! Similar to our feathered friend, someone does have to find, buy, prepare and serve the food, and then clean up the mess! The full responsibility for all this may rest on you, or perhaps you share these responsibilities with others in your home. Nevertheless, the task can be overwhelming, especially if you have several mouths to feed or have special dietary needs to consider. Perhaps you do not have many culinary skills or don't even like to cook.

Listen to this story about Bonny, who was a *Your Home Matters* class participant:

"When Bonny married, she was used to fending for herself when it came to eating at home. With the comings and goings of her family members, regular cooking and meals were not the norm. Both she and her husband thought the other would be doing the cooking when they got married. When she realized that this was going to be in her job description, she knew that she needed help! Being a woman of faith, she asked God to give her the desire and ability to cook. To the delight of both she and her husband, Bonny has become an amazing cook, and she loves doing it! At the time of this writing, she has personally compiled three cookbooks, which she has generously shared with

her friends and family. The only complaint I have ever heard from her hus-
band was that, because Bonny is always cooking new things, he hopes some
of his favorites will show up on the dinner table a second time!"

What I like the most about this story is how Bonny's faith helped her in a very practical way. Her willingness to do something she had no expertise in or desire for shows her willingness to try, trust and be taught. God not only helped her cook for her husband and now her family, He surprised her by giving her an amazing talent to become a most excellent cook!

"SOS" prayer

There are several things you can do to relieve this stress and bring some fun and excitement into meal preparation. But if you identify with Bonny, why not take a few minutes to offer your own "SOS"-type prayer to God? Ask Him to give you the ability and desire to feed your family well—and to help you even learn to enjoy it! Watch with great expectation as your stress turns into anticipation, trusting God in this practical way.

The worst part of cooking for me is trying to figure out what to make for dinner. I am not alone in this; the syndrome is known as the "five o'clock rush hour". You rush to the grocery store and comb the isles in search of something for dinner. Perhaps for you it is more like rushing to the drive-through. Either way, dinner-time can be stressful!

Food storage

Food is stored in three different areas: your freezer, refrigerator and pantry. (If you store food in some of your cupboards that is your pantry.) You will apply The System to these areas too: "throw away, put away, and give away". If you have excess food, share it with someone. Perhaps a hungry adult child who has left the nest, someone you personally know, or a local food bank that would benefit from your food gift. Sharing always holds blessings for you as well as the recipient.

Making an extra sandwich blessed a homeless man. When a mom was asked by her children how they could help a homeless man they saw every morning on their way to school, they decided together to make extra sandwiches the next morning, and then they gave them to him. Both the givers and the receiver were very blessed by this "simple" act of being prepared to share what they had.

Getting started

You might want to clean and organize your freezer, refrigerator, and pantry on three different days to make this task more manageable — or you could work shelf by shelf, until you get the job done. Consistency will pay off and bring with it a wonderful sense of accomplishment. There are no rules; find what works best for you. I want to share with you something that happened to me, and I hope it might help you to feel not so overwhelmed with your freezer!

A chilling experience

The previous owners of a home my husband and I purchased had lived there for over fifty years. They were an elderly couple and left several freezers in the home that we needed to dispose of. The biggest one, a chest-type freezer, was full to the brim with frozen food! There was no part of me that was looking forward to tackling this unbelievable job, but I knew I had to do it. Donning our rubber gloves with the garbage can close by, my granddaughter Jenny and I started the task. The couple had been one of the town's morticians, which made Jenny feel uneasy. With a worried expression on her pale little face, she handed me a packaged marked "back bones." I reassured her that they were from a butcher and were used for making soup. As we dug and dumped, we were seeing a whole new level of "freezer burn." Some of the meat labels dated back to 1970! Although we did not find the original Swanson's TV dinner (1953), we did find one that was forty years old!

By the time we finished the job, we had filled two large, rolling garbage cans to the brim. I did not sleep well that night, wondering if the garbage collectors might peek inside the cans and refuse to empty them! What if they missed our house or an animal got into the garbage cans and scattered the contents all over our yard or our neighbor's yard? Or what if it ate some of that mystery meat and died!? Sleep finally came, and early in the morning I woke to the noise of the garbage collectors.

Taking care not to be seen, I peeked through the curtains. The garbage cans were covered with condensation from the thawing food inside. Oh dear, I hoped they would not come to the door and start asking questions! I continued to watch with relief as I saw the last bit of that once frozen mess tip into the garbage truck. With a deep sigh I could finally relax. With that came thankfulness to God for our dear garbage men — and for that awful job finally being finished!

I am thankful that my freezer is not that bad, and I am guessing that neither is yours!

Freezer

Step by step process to clean and organize your freezer:

- You may want to unplug your freezer if you anticipate this job taking a long time, but it is not necessary for cleaning.
- Unload your freezer, placing the food on a counter top or table. Group like items together. You will make your freezer inventory before returning the food to your freezer.
- Open the door and remove the plastic guard at the bottom of the freezer and wash it off. Vacuum the coil that the guard covers before replacing it. This will help your appliance to run more efficiently and should be done once a year.
- Wipe around the doors, making sure the seal is free from residue. This will preserve the life of the seal and also help with efficiency.
- Throw away anything that you can't identify or know you will never use; recycle glass and plastic containers. We all hate to be wasteful, but after organizing and creating a freezer inventory, you will find that wasting food will be a thing of the past.
- Working shelf by shelf, remove the food, and then wipe down each with a cloth dampened with warm water. Carefully remove any bins and wash them in warm water (hot water may make them crack). Replace each rack, shelf and bin as you clean it. This way you will know exactly where they fit.

- Now that your freezer is clean, you are ready to place the food back in it. But before you do, grab pencil and paper and create a "freezer inventory" by writing down categories (see list below). Be sure to leave space under each group to write down the food items you currently have. You will use this along with refrigerator and pantry inventories in meal planning and for making your grocery shopping list. A legal-size pad works well for this purpose, and be sure to use a pencil so you can erase items as you use them (You can also create these inventory lists on your mobile phone.). Categories: meat, seafood, vegetables, fruit, bread, leftovers, desserts, and "misc." for sauces, grated cheese, etc.; add any other items you might have.

By organizing your food in groups on specific shelves you will know what you have and be able to easily find items. If your freezer is a pull-out drawer or in the top part of your refrigerator, designate "areas" for your categories. It might take you a while to figure out what works best for you; just keep tweaking until you like it.

MY FREEZER ARRANGEMENT, to give you an example:

- *Top shelf:* leftovers in labeled individual microwave containers at eye level to eat for lunch or a quick dinner; pizza ingredients— I use a large zipper-type plastic bag (2-gallon) for homemade pizza ingredients, like dough enough for one pizza (in smaller zip plastic bags), homemade pizza sauce (in snack-size zip bags), browned sausage, pepperoni, leftover cooked vegetables, and pineapple cut in small pieces. (When I have leftovers that would be good on a pizza, I throw them in that bag. This way they do not go to waste, and I can find them when I am ready to make pizza.)

- *Second shelf:* meat. I buy meat in bulk and store it in "meal size" portions, flattening each packet to take up less space before I place it in the freezer. This process will also save you from defrosting more meat than you need.

Mark each item on your freezer inventory sheet as you place the food in the freezer. You can mark your inventory sheet like this: chicken breasts | | | (indicating 3 meals), ground beef | | | | | | (indicating 6 meals), pork chops | | (indicating 2 meals), etc. Erase a mark as you use the item. By carefully marking what you have in your freezer you will know what meals you can make, and you will no longer have to dig through frozen food trying to see what you have.

On this shelf I also place seafood (fish, shrimp, scallops, etc.) in a 2-gallon zipper-type bag. Keeping these items together makes locating each one easy. This is especially helpful when making seafood enchiladas, for which I use a combination.

- *Third shelf:* bread and frozen vegetables. Because there are now just two of us at home, I freeze all bread to keep it fresh. As long as it is sliced, it is easy to separate what is needed. I place hoagie-type rolls in baggies with enough for one meal, again making it easy to grab just what I need. When I have just a few slices or pieces of a bread item, they are placed in a large zippered bag. This keeps them from getting lost or freezer-burned and also makes them accessible, so I can use them up. I also use them to make bread crumbs, bread pudding or dressing/stuffing.

- *Fourth shelf (really a bin):* fruit and desserts. Cutting cakes, pies, etc., into individual servings or just enough for my husband and me helps with portion control! I wrap each item in foil (marking contents) or place in marked freezer bags. In the summer I remove ice cream bars, etc., from the box and then place them in a 2-gallon zippered bag. This keeps them fresher, and it's easy to see what is on hand. I do this with Christmas cookies too, wrapping each type together so the flavors don't mix. When making pie crusts, it is just as easy to make several and then freeze them. Because I make them in disposable pie pans, they stack nicely; place a piece of waxed paper in-between each crust so you can remove just one crust easily. Several will fit in a 1-gallon zip-type bag. Place Graham cracker/ cookie crusts in another 1-gallon zip bag and stack on top of the other crusts to keep them from crumbling. If you buy crusts, place them in a zip-type bag to keep them nice and fresh; the packaging they come in can let air in and eventually cause freezer burn.

- *Door shelves/bins:* miscellaneous items like grated cheeses and grated parmesan flakes in one, bread crumbs and wheat germ in another, and juice and ice packs together.

I freeze lemon and other types of juices in ice cube trays. Once they are frozen, I tip them out into a zippered bag and mark what they are. This also works well with leftover chicken or beef broth.

When you keep items in the same place in your freezer, you will be able to find them. You will also know when you need to add that item to your shopping list! If you are interested, you can go online for general information on how long specific items can remain frozen. Foods that are frozen too long lose their flavor, texture, and nutritional value but are usually not unsafe to eat. Check your refrigerator or freezer manual for suggested temperatures for maximum efficiency.

Refrigerator

Before you start to clean out your fridge, grab another sheet of paper and a pencil and make your "refrigerator inventory". Make categories with what you have in your fridge, leaving space under each group to add your items. Keep this with your freezer inventory.

Categories: beverages, dairy, cold cuts, condiments, fruits, vegetables, miscellaneous

Step by Step process to clean and organize your refrigerator:

- Throw away anything that has expired or has turned green and is not a vegetable! Recycle glass and plastic containers.
- Combine small amounts of the same or similar items if you can, to free up space.
- With the door open, remove the plastic guard at the bottom of the fridge and wash it off. Vacuum the coil that the guard covers before replacing it. This will help your appliance to run more efficiently and should be done once a year.
- Wipe around the doors, making sure the seal is free from residue. This will preserve the life of the seal and also help with efficiency.
- Working your way from top to bottom, remove food and wipe each shelf down. If you need to, remove the shelf and take it to the sink to wash. Remember to use warm, not hot, water. Replace each shelf as you go so you return it to its right place.
- Replace the food in groups that make sense to you, like salad dressings in one area, condiments together, sandwich ingredients together in a container you can easily remove. Keeping your items in the same place will help you to know what you have and to avoid buying duplicates.

- Wipe off the top of the refrigerator and the doors. If your appliances are stainless steel, you might want to use something like the Weiman brand of stainless steel cleaner; it cleans streak-free, is inexpensive, and can be found in most grocery stores in the cleaning-product aisle.
- Wiping the shelves and outside doors periodically or after you shop will keep your fridge clean.

MY FREEZER ARRANGEMENT, to give you an example:

(Arrange your items in a way that makes sense to you)

- *Top shelf:* I make rows, front to back, of milk and rice milk; then coffee creamer, half-and-half and heavy cream; then iced tea, juice and Gatorade. The rows on each shelf are not necessary, but they help me know what I have at a glance, and I can easily direct others to an item.
- *Second shelf:* I make a row of jams and jellies; of olives, pickles, and jars of peppers; and of cottage cheese, yogurt and sour cream.
- *Top small drawer:* cheeses, freshly grated parmesan and feta cheese. I use a zip-type bag for sauce packets from restaurants: hot sauce, soy sauce, etc. This is a good place to store a container for sandwich items.
- *Third shelf:* items that I want to use soon, like leftovers that I don't freeze, perishable fruit, and eggs stored in their cartons.
- *Fourth shelf:* canned drinks. Because these are heavy, I like to store them on the bottom shelf; I place them in rows of like kind.
- *Top and bottom vegetable bins:* salad items and vegetables to be used soon in the top. Vegetables that can be stored longer — potatoes, onions, carrots, cabbage, etc. — are in the bottom bin.
- *First door shelf:* salad dressings (I can grab and return them in one swoop).
- *Second door shelf:* condiments, grouping mustards together, mayo, ketchup, relish, etc.
- *Third door shelf:* sauces used for cooking.
- *Fourth door shelf:* ice cream toppings, lemon and lime juice.

Pantry

This could get messy and take some time. If your time is limited, you might want to work shelf by shelf. Be sure to make a "pantry inventory" as you go, just as you did for your freezer and refrigerator. Leave space under each category to write your items, and keep this list with your other inventories.

Categories:
- Paper products: cups, plates, napkins, foil, baggies, etc.
- Breakfast: cereal, pancake mix, syrup
- Beverage: coffee, tea, hot cocoa, etc.
- Cooking: rice, pasta, seasoning packets, broths, vinegars, oils, etc.
- Baking: flour, sugar, mixes, chocolate chips, nuts, coconut, corn syrup, molasses, etc.
- Snacks: nuts, dried fruit, candy, etc.
- Canned food

I either group or place each category on a shelf or half of a shelf, placing heavier items like canned food, pet foods, and extra supplies on a lower shelf or in bins on the floor. I also have an area for supplies I might need to replenish because I use them regularly.

Step by step process to clean and organize your pantry:
- Working your way from top to bottom, remove everything from each shelf and then wipe it down with warm, soapy water.
- Dry each shelf before returning food.
- Place your food items in the categories you have on your inventory list, grouping like items together.
- If you are feeling extra ambitious, you could paint or put shelf paper on your shelves (use the kind you can wipe down).

Extra step:

I wanted to show a picture of my pantry and how I grouped items when teaching a *Your Home Matters* class, so I made pantry signs out of card stock for each section, attaching them to the wire shelving. I really liked how the signs looked and ended up leaving them. This is a good way to help family members know where to return items.

Tips:

- To save time when baking, store baking soda, baking powder, salt, vanilla, yeast, and any other item you use together in recipes in a removable bin/basket or container, and keep on your baking shelf.

- Place your baking spices in that same container or in a separate one; keep on your baking shelf.

- Transfer rice and pastas to glass jars to keep them fresh. They look nice too and help you see how much you have.

- Remove snack items from their boxes if they are individually wrapped, and store them in a bin or large zip-type bag.

- Store nuts and dried fruit in mason jars with lids on your snack shelf to encourage healthy choices.

- Make your snack shelf high if you have little ones.

- Hide special snacks inside an empty soda cracker box or something your family would not normally reach for. Just remember where you stashed them!

- Mark ingredients that you need for specific meals or desserts with an "off limits" or "beware" sign.

- If you stock up on canned food items, arrange by expiration dates (or place the newest ones in the back of the row) so you can use the oldest first.

- Place canned food items by rows and types for easy retrieval.

- Tidy up your pantry periodically to keep it from becoming a big mess. I try to do this when I am putting items away after grocery shopping.

A friend of mine gave me a loaf of delicious, warm, friendship bread and a "starter" so I could make some too. I had no idea how much my life was about to change! True, every ten days we would enjoy another loaf of this warm, yummy bread, but I now felt like I had a part-time job! I had to do something with this starter just about every day. There was one day for which the recipe said, "Let the starter rest today." I loved that day: not only did the starter get to rest, so did I! Every ten days, when it was time to make the bread, I had to locate and gather everything I needed. Finally I decided to store these ingredients together. This simple step saved me so much time! All I had to do was grab the container from my pantry to make the bread. When I finally decided to quit this part-time job, I replaced each ingredient back in my pantry where it normally lived and threw the starter away! I was very careful after that to avoid making eye contact with anyone with a friendship-bread starter to give away, unless I was up for the task!

Meal planning and grocery shopping

Throughout our lives we will experience different seasons, with some seeming longer than others. If you are in a season that seems to never end, take heart: it will not last forever! My "seasons" of grocery shopping have changed over the years; try to identify what season you are currently in.

Newly married: no money, no clue and a hungry husband to feed; missing Mom's cooking!

Starting a family: I remember my hubby saying "Hurry home!" as I headed out the door. Yeah, right, I thought… Grocery shopping was my big night out, and I had no intention of rushing. Besides that, I had to strategically time my return home, ensuring all small children were in bed! I am quite certain that this is when I developed an appreciation for soft music (the kind I made fun of as a teen). During this season I became proficient in making a list and using a calculator; I had to make both food and money "s t r e t c h". If this is your current season and you shop with a small child, your task is not for the weak or faint in heart! It always amazes me just how far those little arms can reach, even with the child strapped securely in the shopping cart. Have you ever watched a mother bird feed her young? That's how I felt with a house full of hungry teenagers. Just like that mama bird, I always seemed to be flying off to the store to find more food — and then I watched it disappear all too quickly!

It was quite obvious to everyone around her that this mommy was frustrated while shopping with her toddler. Those who were close to her in the checkout line could hear her gently repeating, "It's OK, Barbara, we will be home in just a few minutes." A man stopped her on her way out the door and commended her on her patience with "Barbara," her active toddler. She sheepishly replied, "Oh, her name is Emma I'm Barbara!"

During this season my lack of planning landed me in the grocery store way too often. Picking up extra items here and there also resulted in my spending too much money. I decided to take a challenge and implemented shopping for two weeks at a time and then eventually just once a month. This was not an easy task, and it usually took several hours to plan and then to do the shopping. I would scour through recipes, plan meals with what I already had and eventually compile a list of what I needed to purchase. I soon realized that the payoff was well worth it. I now had more time every day, and I was saving a considerable amount of money, but what really excited me: I started to enjoy cooking! I loved knowing that I had at least 14 meals (shopping every two weeks) or approximately 25 meals (shopping monthly and eating leftovers on weekends) that I could make having 90% of the ingredients on hand. This eliminated those rushed trips to the grocery store before I could make dinner. I did have to make occasional "extra" trips to pick up milk and some fresh fruit and vegetables when shopping on a monthly basis, but those trips were infrequent. This might not fit into your budget or even be of interest to you, but if you would like to save both time and money, I encourage you to at least shop on a weekly basis. Unless you are extremely disciplined and intentional in what you purchase and can refrain from purchasing items you don't need, you are probably spending more money than you would if you shopped weekly.

The Empty-nester: This is my current season. This was a hard adjustment at first: I felt kind of sad because I was missing our children, or I cooked way too much food! I am glad to report that this sadness did not last very long. Now I occasionally cook for a crowd and almost every night for my husband and myself, and I love it! Even cooking for two, I will still make full recipes and freeze a portion. On a busy night these are "treasures" in the freezer or "bonus" meals that are a benefit from cooking once and eating twice. Meal planning and grocery shopping go hand in hand. You will be amazed at the time and money you will save with just a little planning.

Grocery list

It is important to devise a plan that works for you and fits the season that you are in. Before making your grocery list, it is helpful to know what you already have on hand. This is when those inventory lists you made for your freezer, refrigerator and pantry will serve you well.

Ready to start?

- Grab your inventory lists and a blank sheet of paper and mark it "Meals."

- Grab your calendar too, so you will know if there are any nights you might not have to cook dinner and what days an easy meal would work best.

- Number how many meals you need to plan and coincide with your weekly, bi-monthly or monthly grocery-shopping plan.

- Write down meals that you can make from what you already have on hand.

- Add any additional meals that you would like to make. Trying new recipes will keep meals interesting — especially for the cook!

- Grab another sheet of paper and mark it "Grocery Shopping List."

- Check to see what ingredients you will need to purchase for each recipe and meal you have listed; add them to your shopping list. This step will keep you from the frustration of the "missing ingredient" that either makes you change what you want to fix or forces you to substitute ingredients.

- Group the items on your list either by store, category, or aisle location. This will save your feet—and time!—since you won't have to return to an aisle several times. If you go to more than one store, write down what you want to purchase at each one.

Shopping

- When shopping, mark off items as you find them and circle any item on your list that you could not find or did not buy because of quality or price, etc. Then you will know what you still need to purchase.

- Make adjustments to your meal list if your store has a sale on a particular item. You might even be able to incorporate the item into several meals, saving even more time and money. For example, if there is a sale on roast beef, you could make several meals: roast, chili, beef stroganoff or beef stew. Buy a larger roast and prepare what you would need for each meal, freezing each portion in zip-type bags. Mark the meal on the label and on your meal list, so you don't forget what you plan on making.

- After your shopping is completed and you return home from the store, add each item you purchased to the appropriate inventory list, and jot down any other meals you think of while putting your food away.

- Taking the time to divide food up into meal portions right after returning from shopping will save you so much time later during the five o'clock rush hour!

- This is also a good time to wipe down your fridge shelves and straighten up the pantry, if you can.

- If there are any meals that you did not make and you still have the ingredients when the time comes for your next shopping trip, you can add these "bonus meals" to your next "meal list".

Tips:

- If you are pressed for time, you can easily update your inventory lists later by looking at your store receipts—even from the couch!

- When you do not have the time to separate your meat into meal portions, place it in the fridge and plan to do that the next day, instead of freezing the whole amount.

- Remember that the time you spend in planning and preparation will always save you more time, probably when you need it the most!

- I have recently transferred my inventory lists to my phone, with the help of some free phone applications. My meal list in particular is like money in the bank to me. Knowing that I have what I need to make several meals helps me to breathe easier and enjoy meal preparation. By taking a quick look at my meal list when I am out, I can easily decide what I want to make for dinner. If I am not sure whether I have all the ingredients, I can check my inventory lists before I head home. This eliminates the meal selection by default or having to radically adjust a recipe to fit the ingredients I have on hand. It took quite a bit of time for me to add this information to my phone but not much time to keep it current.

- This can also easily be accomplished by keeping your inventory and meal lists with you, maybe in a spiral notebook.

If cooking once and eating at least twice appeals to you, here are some suggestions to get you started:

- *Chili:* Make your favorite version, doubling the recipe, and you can dine on: chili, chili-topped baked potatoes, taco salad (heat one cup chili and stir it into salad; top with tortilla chips just before serving), chili in cups. For the last suggestion: press a refrigerator or homemade biscuit dough into a greased muffin tin, spoon in some chili, sprinkle with grated cheese, and bake at 400° for 10 minutes or until biscuit is done and chili is bubbling. My kids loved these, and they also freeze well and can be heated in the microwave or oven.

- *Chicken:* Bake several breasts, thighs, or a whole chicken, shred cooked meat, and freeze in zip-type bags to make: your favorite chicken casserole, chicken tacos, or chicken tortilla soup.

- *Beef roast:* Purchase a large roast, cooking a portion for a roast beef dinner, shred extra cooked meat, and freeze in zip-type bags, and you can make soups or shredded beef Mexican dishes. You can trim off and cube some of the meat before cooking to make beef stroganoff or stew.

- *Extra fish or vegetables*: Grill and you can top off a salad to serve for dinner, use on pizza or make into sandwiches.

- *Meatballs:* Make up a batch, bake and freeze to make: Italian dishes with pasta, sub sandwiches, sweet and sour meatballs, or for an appetizer.

Maintenance – Keep it tidy and organized!

Maintenance – After grocery shopping, remember to try to wipe down and organize the refrigerator, freezer and pantry before putting items away. You don't have to become obsessive about this – but don't neglect it either. Otherwise all of your hard work will need to be repeated, not just maintained.

In this chapter

You discovered ways to keep everyone fed without becoming fed-up with the process! By applying these simple but life changing strategies and tips – your meal planning and grocery shopping stress will melt away!

> *People do not live by bread alone, but by every word that*
> *comes from the mouth of God.*
> ~ Matthew 4:4

In the next chapter

Get ready to reclaim your laundry room and make that area more efficient and cheerful. You can finally catch up on your laundry in just a few hours by taking a little trip! You will also learn how to launder just about everything, and keep more money in your pocket – more money than you'll ever find in the pockets of the clothes you are laundering!

Chapter 10

Laundry
It seems to multiply when you're not looking!

Scripture
Create in me a clean heart, O God.
Renew a loyal spirit within me.
~ Psalm 51:10

If it is your job to make sure everyone has clean clothes to wear, you don't have an easy one! Overseeing the continuous transformation of mounds of dirty laundry into ready-to-wear clothing is a job that's hard to get a handle on. My prayer for you is that your laundry-related stress will be lowered as you move toward doable solutions that work for you. Who knows? You might even enjoy yourself while you are at it! I hope so!

In this chapter you will find help in:
- reclaiming your laundry room
- making the area/room you do laundry in more efficient and cheerful
- enjoying finally catching up on all that laundry
- how to launder just about everything
- keeping money in your pocket — much more than what you find in pockets while doing laundry!

Hope your team wins!

Before we get started, I want to share a funny story. A frazzled woman was in her basement doing laundry. As she busily loaded her washing machine, the exposed pipe above her began to drip on her head. Her annoyance gave way to solution as she spied her son's football helmet on the floor and she put it on. Before closing the lid to the machine, she decided to take off her dress and throw that in the washer too. "Hope your team wins!" the forgotten furnace repairman said as he quickly grabbed his tool box and bolted for the stairway.

Beware when you are in the "laundry zone" and up to your neck in laundry!

Ready to start?

We will cover two areas in this chapter: first, the area or room where you do your laundry; and second, the actual laundry. Maybe you have a specific room for laundry, or perhaps your washer and dryer are in a hallway, the garage, or the basement, like the lady in my story. The location of your laundry area will contribute to how much clutter ends up there. Laundry areas by the back door seem to be the worst for collecting unwanted items.

Step by step

You are going to apply The System (Chapter 1) to this area. You might need a large garbage bag for all the junk you find! Again, be ruthless; you have my permission! Realize that there is risk involved for family members who use this space to dump their things. Place items that you or your family will need to put away in another box—be sure to put them away later, so you won't get distracted. Rearrange or move any large items that you don't want stored in your laundry room to another area, like a garage, to deal with later. If your laundry area is in the garage or basement, move anything that is not related to laundry to another area in the garage or basement. Clearing this area will help the laundry process get done more quickly and give you more room to sort and fold. Think about how nice it will be not to have to look at all that clutter anymore!

Now that your laundry area is cleaned out, here are some things to consider.

Things to consider:

- If you do not have cabinets above your washer/dryer, can you hang a shelf or shelves? Plastic-covered wire shelving works well here; it is easy to wipe down, and you can hang hangers from it too.

- Using expansion shower curtain rods is another way to create a hanging area. Taking the time to hang clothes as they come out of the dryer will save you time and prevent wrinkles. If this will not work in your area, maybe an over-the-door hanging system will. One laundry room I saw had a bunk-bed ladder suspended horizontally from the ceiling. This provided a great space to hang items and looked very cool when the laundry was put away.

- If you use economy-size containers of laundry products, decant them into a more manageable-sized container, and store your main supply where you have room.

- Keep your iron (if you use one) and a small mending kit handy to help keep these tasks from piling up and all clothing ready to wear.

Extra step:

- Now that your laundry area is neat and tidy, why not decorate it too? A new coat of paint will always "freshen" things up.

- Whimsical works well in a laundry room, making you smile and brightening your laundry day! Decorate with something fun or quirky that you might not use in another area of your home. This is a great place to hang pictures of your family — hopefully, seeing their smiling faces will help you to not grumble while doing their laundry.

- Frame a Scripture here to lift your spirits!

- Is this area a good place for a family calendar?

- Lighting is important: cleaning a light fixture or replacing the bulb to a higher wattage (if recommended for that fixture) will make a big difference.

- How about some music? It is said to calm a savage beast!

Maintenance – Keeping it tidy and organized!

- Consider bolting the door! If this is not practical, declare this area "off limits" to anything other than laundry. You probably will have to enforce this law with consequences for violators — perhaps suggesting that they do the laundry!

- Keep a small garbage can or container handy for dryer lint, and throw away things you find in pockets.

- A throw rug placed in front of your dryer will catch wet laundry. And those pieces of lint, paper, etc., that fall out when you open the dryer door. Just shake the rug out when needed to keep your room tidy.

- A washable mat in front of the washer will also catch drips of soap. White is a good color if you use bleach, otherwise your rug might acquire some white spots (the voice of experience!).

- Keep a stain-removing chart, lint brush, and a small scrubbing brush nearby. Don't forget a piggy bank for all the money you find!

- If your laundry room serves more than one purpose, provide a bin for each family member to keep personal items in, similar to what we discussed in the entrance, media and living room chapters.

- Keep some rags handy to wipe down your machines after use.

- Run 1 cup of vinegar through your washing machine periodically to clean out soap build-up — see the recipe for deep-cleaning your machine and the one for homemade laundry soap later on in this chapter.

- Laundry sorters will save you time. They come in varied sizes; measure and see if one will fit in your laundry area.

It will all come out in the wash — now, let's get to that laundry!

Attitude is everything; maintaining a good one toward laundry is a challenge, especially when you feel overwhelmed. I remember reading about the woman in Proverbs, Chapter 31 and her servant girls (the last part of Verse 15). Wouldn't it be nice to have a team working with you to get the work done? Then I realized that I do have a team of "servants" helping me. Perhaps naming them might help me to view them in a more personal way: Wilma the Washing Machine, Doris the Dryer, and Dishwasher Dottie. They are the best kind of servants too: they just do their work! Still not convinced? Imagine lugging your laundry down to the river to wash it and hanging it over tree branches to dry! My grandma used a wringer-washer, which looked dangerous, and she hung her clothes out on a line to dry. I love the smell of laundry that has been hung outside on a line, but I am thankful that I can get my laundry done quickly, even on a rainy day. We truly are fortunate to have our "servants"! If you are still not convinced, give them the week off and get back to me. ☺

You can apply the system to your actual laundry on a continual basis as you:
- Throw away what is no longer useful.
- Put away out-of-season clothing (less clothing in closets equals less laundry).
- Give away what is still useful to family, friends, consignment shops, or a Goodwill-type of store. *Note:* Do not donate stained or unusable clothing. Your local store will appreciate that.

How do you do laundry?

Is there always a load in the dryer calling your name? Do you do laundry every day? Or do you prefer washing several loads one or two times a week? Either way, I encourage you to do what works best for you! This can change when your season of life changes, so be flexible.

When my kids were growing up, I usually did laundry on Mondays and Thursdays, with an occasional load of towels in-between. It was important for me to complete the laundry process; the laundry was not really done until everything was put away! If your stress level was high for this area, make some changes to lower your stress.

Sorting is one way to preserve your clothing by washing like colors and types of material together. It is best to wash whites, bright colors, darks, permanent press, work clothes, delicate apparel, towels, and sheets in separate loads.

Here are the recommended temperatures to wash typical items:

- whites: hot water/cold rinse
- bright colors: cold water/cold rinse
- darks: either warm or cold water/cold rinse
- permanent press: warm or cold water/cold rinse
- heavily soiled or work clothes: warm or hot water/cold rinse, using long cycle
- delicate: cold water/cold rinse; or hand wash and dry flat, or hang to dry
- towels: hot/warm water/cold rinse
- sheets: hot/warm water/ cold rinse

Cold water will preserve the colors in your clothes and will keep blue and black jeans from fading so fast. Add $\frac{1}{2}$ - 1 cup of vinegar to your cold wash the first time you wash these items, or for items that will bleed, and be sure to wash them separately. Run an extra rinse cycle when your washer is empty to remove any color residue that could get on your next load. You can dissolve dry detergent in 1 cup of warm water and add to the cold water load to insure that all of your laundry soap dissolves — only necessary if you see undissolved soap on your clothes when the cycle is completed.

Cold/Warm water is best for permanent press and lightly soiled clothes.

Hot water kills bacteria and is recommended for sheets and towels. Add $\frac{1}{8}$ - $\frac{1}{4}$ cup of liquid disinfectant in the wash cycle for sheets and towels if a family member is sick — or during flu season.

After sorting your laundry, launder each load according to the recommended water temperature.

Overloading your machines will make them work too hard. You don't want your maids to decide to quit on you! If you overload your washing machine, your laundry will not get clean, and this can cause it to smell bad too. When washing comforters, throw rugs or heavy items, be sure to balance your load. Otherwise you may find that your washer has moved to the middle of the room and your clothes are still soapy and wet at the end of the cycle.

Overloading your dryer will cause your items to wrinkle unnecessarily and can cause an unpleasant odor in your clothes, especially towels. It is better to have two loads of the same type of clothes than to have to launder them over again.

Folding your clothes as soon as your dryer stops will help you finish your laundry in half the time and keep your clothes from unnecessary wrinkling. Because your dryer does not completely cool between loads, drying loads of laundry back to back will save energy and money. Engaging the buzzer on your machine will remind you when your clothes are dry. Carrying a small timer in your pocket will do the same thing. Keep those machines/servants on task—they will get their break, and so will you, when the laundry is done!

Overwhelmed? Feel like you will never see the laundry room floor again?

When this is your reality or you just have more than a normal amount of laundry, make a trip to your local Laundromat. If this makes no sense to you when you have a perfectly good washer and dryer in your home, hear me out! Although it will cost you extra money, you will save time and shake that overwhelmed feeling. Can you imagine having all of your laundry done? What an incredible feeling! Immediately make some changes to avoid getting into this situation again. Learning to manage your laundry will keep your stress level down, give you a great sense of accomplishment, and keep all of your clothing available on a regular basis.

Another time you might want to load the car up and head to the Laundromat is when you return home from a family vacation. A week's worth of dirty laundry for every family member, coupled with your current laundry, is hard for anyone to manage efficiently. Give yourself a break and get it all done in a few hours! We have on occasion caught up on our laundry while traveling. If this is a viable option for you, get the whole family involved; they will see first hand how laundry is done. Ice cream cones for all might be a fun treat when the laundry is completed!

Several members in your household?

- Designate baskets for dirty laundry in each bedroom.

- Expect able family members to deliver their baskets to the laundry room when needed.

- Require these family members to put their clean clothes away and completely clear the laundry area.

- Beware: your kids may try the "leave the laundry in the basket trick", which is OK if they want to wear their clothes right from the basket (although hanging and putting them away is usually preferred). Warn them that the authorities (that would be you) will be called in when clean clothes end up with dirty ones piled on top of them. Never wash a clean item if at all possible – I think it is against the law!

- Resist the temptation to let your laundry room become the family clothes closet.

- Consider assigning laundry duty days to age-appropriate children. You might be thinking this is not possible or not worth the effort. It is possible! Who knows? When you take the time and effort to teach your children to do their own laundry, they might even do yours too! If this scares you, just have them launder their own clothes! Remember: you are teaching them life skills and responsibility. I am amazed at how many adults I have met who have never learned how to do laundry. If that is you, now you know how! Small children can do this too; with your assistance and wild cheering, they will love being a helper!

Too many clothes!

Most of us have too many clothes and still complain about having nothing to wear. We could probably go months without laundering if we wore everything in our closets just once. If you pare down on clothes, you will naturally have less laundry. Traveling has shown me that you can wear a lot of your clothing more than once. Jeans can be worn several times before they need to be laundered. Sometimes I think we wash the life right out of our clothes. Better to wear them out by wearing them instead of by washing them!

More tips:

- Add 1 cup of vinegar to the rinse cycle to ensure all the soap rinses out.

- Add ½ cup of baking soda to the rinse cycle to soften your towels.

- Use bleach sparingly as it weakens the fibers in fabric.

- For stubborn stains, spray your favorite stain remover on the spot and then sprinkle a little baking soda on top. The foaming action from the baking soda will lift the stain from the fiber of the material. Let this mixture sit for just a few minutes and then launder. (Thanks, Stacey!)

- For stain removal on the go, gently rub Lava soap (bar) on the stain to lift it. Pat with a wet cloth and you can continue to wear the clothing spot-free! Do not use this method on delicate clothing.

- If you have a front-loading washing machine, remember to use only HE (high efficiency) laundry soap, and don't use too much. Your soap dispenser might collect water, so empty it out when you are finished — if it is removable. If you leave the door propped open, the large gasket around the door can air dry; that will keep your washer smelling fresh.

- Cut down on the amount of soap you use in all of your appliances, a repair man told me, and your machines will last longer — even your dishwasher.

- If you must use dryer sheets, cut them in half; this will save you money and help to reduce residue build-up on the inside of your dryer.

- Dryer balls can be used instead of dryer sheets. This is recommended for heavy items only; they might damage more delicate ones.

- Do sheets tangle in your dryer? Throw three new tennis balls in with your sheets; the balls will help distribute the load. (Note: they are a little noisy.) I keep mine hidden away in the drawer beneath my dryer, using them for this purpose only.

- Keep your lint screen clean after each load and your clothes will dry faster—and your dryer won't have to work so hard.

- Use medium heat on your dryer (except for towels) to keep your clothes in good shape longer.

- Using towels more than once will drastically reduce your laundry. Let them dry out completely after using, outside if you can.

- When drying towels, move them to the dryer as soon as they are washed. They will take on an odor if left in the washer too long, which will require you to launder them again.

- If your towels continue to have an odor, add 1 cup vinegar and ½ cup baking soda to the rinse cycle. If they still smell, soak them in the washing machine with this mixture for 1 hour and then launder. Still smell? Soak overnight.

- You can hang a shirt or a blouse on a hanger outside (out of direct sunlight) to freshen. This will cut down on your laundry and give longevity to your clothes. This works great for dry-clean only clothes between dry-cleanings.

Recipe for laundry soap, saving you $$$

1 bar Fels Naptha soap* **, grated (about 2 cups)
1 cup Borax
1 cup washing soda (Arm & Hammer makes it)
* or equivalent, for you foreign readers
** grate a bar of Ivory soap to make infant laundry detergent

Use 1 Tablespoon for a light load
Use 2 Tablespoons for a large or heavily soiled load.
Front-loading washers: place detergent inside the washing machine.
I double this recipe to yield approximately 100 loads.

A repairman suggested I use 1 cup of Tang orange dry mix instead of buying a special cleaner to remove any smell in my "high efficiency" washing machine. I only needed to do this once and found, as stated before, that propping my door open until the gasket is dry and emptying the water from my soap dispenser keeps my machine smelling fresh.

Recipe to keep your washing machine clean, saving you $$$

This will keep your washing machine clean and sanitized. Clean your machine at regular intervals, based on the amount of usage, and it will last longer.

You will need:
2 cups white vinegar
2 cups bleach

1. Fill your washing machine with hot water and add 2 cups of white vinegar.
2. Allow the machine to agitate for a few minutes to thoroughly mix the vinegar and water; pause the cycle for 1 hour to allow the solution time to clean and disinfect the tub.
3. Resume the cycle.
4. Refill the washer with hot water and add 2 cups bleach, and follow the same process as you did with the vinegar.

Maintenance - Keep it tidy and organized!

Remember to wipe your machines down periodically and apply the machine- cleaning procedures as needed. I like to keep a small container on top of my washing machine where I can toss miscellaneous items that find their way into the laundry area. This is also a great place to look for missing items! Empty once a month.

In this chapter

After you have cleared out your laundry area, I hope you try some of the ideas to make this area a nicer place to do laundry. You learned how to do the laundry – in case you didn't know – and now you can also teach this skill. It is amazing that just by making a few changes, you will reduce your laundry and your stress! I love to meditate on this scripture while doing laundry.

Create in me a clean heart, O God.
Renew a loyal spirit within
~ Psalm 51:10

In the next chapter

You will learn how to clean a bathroom like a pro in 10 minutes (teach this technique to everyone who lives in your home). Wouldn't it be great to keep what you need and use regularly at your fingertips? Once you learn how to do this you will spend less time on your morning bathroom routine!

Chapter 11

Bathroom
Clean one in 10 minutes...

Scripture

Search me, O God, and know my heart; test me and know my
anxious thoughts. Point out anything in me that offends you,
and lead me along the path of everlasting life.
~ Psalm 139:23–24

In this chapter you will find help in:
- how to clean a bathroom like a pro in 10 minutes
- keeping what you need and use regularly at your fingertips
- spending less time on your morning bathroom routine

Ready to start?

Implement The System (Chapter 1) in each one of your bathrooms. Don't know which one to start with? If you are feeling a little overwhelmed, start with the easiest one first; admire your work and then move on to your next bathroom (if you have more than one).

Throw away -
pitch products that are past their prime!

Medicine cabinets: check for expired items and also check to find out where you can safely dispose of expired medicine. Don't flush or toss medicine in the trash; it could leach into water systems and landfills.

Even those who love to pare down tend to hold on to creams and dreams (of what they will do for you) too long; most personal products become less effective overtime. Throwout anything that smells or looks funny or has expired, especially if you have no idea what it was supposed to do for you in the first place! In general, eye make-up is good for six months, foundation for one year, and lipsticks for two years. Preservative-free products degrade more quickly than others. Because lipstick lasts so long, if you have a favorite, you might want to file the name so you can buy it again. Often by the time I have reached the bottom of the tube, I can no longer read the name of the color.

Sticker strategy

Write the month and year that you purchased the make-up on a small sticker or a piece of masking tape, and attach it to the bottom of the jar or tube of make-up. In time, if the item starts looking questionable, you can refer to this date to see if you're in the clear or not. By brushing a clear coat of nail polish over the label, it will repel water.

Put away... everything that belongs in that bathroom. Consider who uses each bathroom, and arrange items for their ease of use. If you have a bathroom that is designated just for guests, a drawer stocked with travel-size essentials is a nice touch (my sister-in-law does this). If your guests share a bath with family members, a small basket placed in that bathroom or in their guest room with essentials is a welcoming touch. Toss everything you find that does not belong in the bathroom into a box to put away later, so you can keep your momentum going.

Give away... usable make-up, perfume, nail polish and products you do not use. If there is a little girl in your life, perhaps you could keep some for dress-up or maybe to use for a costume party. Keep them in a separate make-up bag. Hotel-size shampoos and lotions are perfect for donating to a shelter or a homeless ministry.

Beat the morning rush... If your morning routine finds you rushing in and out of your bathroom, having everything readily available will be a time saver for you. You can arrange everything you use on a small tray and keep it on top of your counter or in a drawer. You no longer have to rummage through your make-up. Having everything you need at your fingertips is a great way to start your day!

If your make-up inventory is large, separate your products— lip colors, shadows, blushes, etc. —by color to help you see all of your options at a glance. Store them conveniently in containers that fit in a drawer to encourage you to use them before you buy more. Choose shallow containers so you can rest your daily make-up tray on top and still shut the drawer. Keep your makeup brushes all by themselves so they don't dust up everything.

When buying drawer organizers, choose ones with several small compartments so it's easier to customize to your needs; these containers are fairly inexpensive. If you are up for the task and want to save money, gather small boxes that will house your make-up and fit in your drawer. Either spray paint them or cover with contact paper or washable wallpaper. You can line each box with disposable paper that can easily be replaced by cutting a piece of paper towel to fit the bottom of each container (you can even staple them together). For you ladies, this could be a fun project to do with your daughter, granddaughter, or any young lady you are mentoring.

Keeping your supplies where you can see them will alert you when they are dwindling. Store your everyday essentials, including cotton balls and swabs, in clear containers within reach. Before you go shopping for containers, consider re-purposing vessels or glass apothecary jars or vases you already have. Bleacher- like units can be purchased or made. They are more commonly used to store spices but can easily be adapted, making it a snap to choose products from your bottles and containers.

Don't hide the T.P. Two perplexities you've probably experienced: (1) you're in your bathroom and you're out of toilet paper, and no one can hear you calling; (2) you're in someone else's bathroom and you realize they are out of toilet paper, and you're not sure what to do! Do you search your host's cupboards or sheepishly cry for help? To avoid both of these scenarios, keep ample rolls in a nearby bin, basket, or reachable cupboard; you and your guests will be glad you did. To prevent the second situation, keep a tissue in your pocket at all times.

❧*The public bathroom experience…*

If you are a woman, it has probably been your experience that, when you have to visit a public bathroom, you usually find a line of ladies, so you smile politely and instinctively take your place in the line. Once it's your turn, you check again for feet under the stall doors… every stall is still occupied! Finally, a door opens and you dash in, nearly knocking down the woman leaving the stall. You get in and find that the door won't latch—it doesn't matter: desperate times call for desperate measures! The dispenser for the "seat covers" (invented by someone's mom, no doubt) is handy, but empty. You would hang your purse on the door hook, if there was one, but there isn't, so you carefully drape it around your neck (your mother taught you to never put it on the floor!), and now you assume "the stance". In this position your aging, toneless thigh muscles begin to shake. You'd love to sit down, but you certainly hadn't taken time to wipe the seat or lay toilet paper on it, so you hold "the stance". To take your mind off your trembling thighs, you reach for what you discover to be the empty toilet paper dispenser. In your mind, you can hear your mother's voice saying, "Honey, if you had tried to clean the seat, you would have known there was no toilet paper!" Now your thighs shake even more. Then you remember the tiny tissue that you blew your nose on yesterday, the one that's still in your purse. (Oh yes, the purse around your neck, that you now have to hold up, trying not to strangle yourself at the same time.) This will have to do, so you crumple it in the puffiest way possible, even though it's still smaller than your thumbnail! Oh dear, someone pushes your door open because the latch doesn't work. The door hits your purse, which is hanging around your neck, and you and your purse topple backward against the tank of the toilet. "Occupied!" you manage to squeak out as you reach for the door, dropping your precious, tiny, crumpled tissue in a puddle on the floor. Now you lose your footing altogether; you slide down directly onto the toilet seat. It is wet, of course. You bolt up, knowing all too well that it's too late. Your bare bottom has made contact with every imaginable germ and life- form on the uncovered seat because you never laid down toilet paper—not that there was any to lay down. You are thinking that your mother would be utterly appalled if she knew, because you're certain her bare bottom never touched a public toilet seat! By this time, the automatic sensor on the back of the toilet is so confused that it flushes, propelling a stream of water like a fire hose against the inside of the bowl that sprays a fine mist of water that covers your back side and runs down your legs and into your shoes. At this point, you give up. You're soaked by the spewing water and the wet toilet seat... You're exhausted... You try to wipe with a gum wrapper you found in your pocket... Then you slink out inconspicuously to the sinks... You can't figure out how to operate the faucets with the automatic sensors, so you wipe your hands with spit and dry your hands on your pants because the paper towel dispenser is empty too! As you walk past the line of women still waiting, you are no longer able to smile politely to them. A kind soul at the very end of the line points out a piece of toilet paper trailing from your shoe. (Where was that when you needed it?) You yank the paper from your shoe, plunk it in the woman's hand and tell her warmly, "You just might need this." As you exit, you spot your hubby, who has long since entered, used, and left the men's restroom. Annoyed, he asks, "What took you so long, and why is your purse hanging around your neck?" This finally explains to men why it really does take us so long. It also answers their other commonly asked questions about why women go to the restroom in pairs: it's obvious you need a friend to hold the door, hang onto your purse, and hand you tissue under the door!

(Unfortunately, the author of this is unknown.)

───────●◆●───────

Stock Up: Stocking up on supplies will save you money and trips to the store. Large containers of shampoo, conditioner, body wash, and liquid soap are much cheaper per ounce than smaller ones. Decant your products into smaller bottles for your shower and to refill travel-size containers. This step will save you from the physical pain of dropping a jumbo-size bottle of shampoo or conditioner on your foot!

Consider the Ceiling: If you need more storage space, look up. Why not take advantage of vertical real estate by hanging a multi-level wire basket, or installing shelving? You can also allow loofahs and bath toys to dry by keeping them in hanging-type storage in your shower.

Create a Caddy: Store hair dryers, curling irons, brushes, and styling products in a caddy or tote with compartments to keep these items neat and together. If you use a tote, hang it on an inside door knob. Wrap the cords of your curling iron and blow dryer loosely, like lassos, to maintain the life of the cord.

Skirt the Issue: If you have a pedestal sink that's not pretty or you need more storage, make a no-sew fabric skirt. I did this and kept an organizing unit on wheels underneath it. I could easily roll it out from under the sink to reach extra hand towels and cleaning supplies, and then roll it back into hiding when finished. In one bathroom my shower curtain was too big; I used what I cut off to make a sink skirt in the same bathroom!

Linens: If you store linens in your bathroom, try rolling your towels; they will stay neat, even when you grab one from the middle. The idea is to store and fold to save you time. Store some face cloths in a drawer or under the sink in a basket to keep them where you use them.

To make a sink skirt

Start with a bed sheet, using the finished hem for the bottom of the skirt. Trim to the needed length and width and "hem" the edges with iron-on hem tape. You could also use a shower curtain, as I did; the water-repellent material is easy to wipe off. Affix industrial-strength Velcro (sold at hardware stores) to the top of the skirt and to the sink where you want to attach the skirt.

Extra step

By adding just a few decorative touches to your bathroom (s), they will not only be organized but beautified too!

Keep your decorations simple and uncluttered so you have less to dust. You can group a few colorful bottles together for a splash of color, or tall glass cylinders that house a collection of shells, etc. Hang a new or different picture on the wall. Across from the toilet is a great place to hang a Scripture, taking advantage of a "captive" audience. Remember: life is too short not to use your good towels, so enjoy!

Cleaning & maintenance

As promised, here is how to clean a bathroom like a pro in just 10 minutes. (Teach some life skills to your kids: photocopy this page and make them responsible for their own bathrooms.)

Mission: Clean bathroom in 10 minutes

- Throw dirty towels in the hall and shake rugs.
- Toss misplaced items in a basket to put away in their designated place (after bathroom is clean).
- Spray cleaner in your shower, tub and toilet (leave on to soak).
- Swiffer or dust any window sill, around tub, picture frames, lights, and anything else that needs dusting.
- Vacuum floor.
- Clean mirror with paper towel / cloth with Windex or water.
- Clean sink and counter top with same cloth you cleaned the mirror with; clean area behind faucets; toss cloth by toilet to use there when finished.
- Toilet: wipe down top first, outside of tank, base, and then the seat/under seat with the tossed cloth.
- Use toilet brush to clean bowl.
- Spray bowl and base with Lysol. (Note: you can remove tough water stains with a pumice stone.)
- Scrub shower and/or tub.
- Mop the floor or wipe down with a cloth, depending on the size of bathroom.
- Put out fresh towels, and you are done!

(Thanks, Anj!)

Tips:

- Take a minute to clean a little after your shower or bath and you will save scrubbing time later.

- Spray a little WD-40 on a paper towel to make your faucets shine. (Be careful not to get any on the floor; it will make it very slippery!)

- CLR (or a similar product) or straight vinegar will remove soap build-up on glass shower doors. Use gloves, and open the window or turn on the fan for ventilation.

- Combine little portions of cosmetics together to make use of every last drop: lip gloss, nail polish.

- Out of eyeliner? Dip your brush into your mascara.

- Wash out your make-up brushes every few months; swirl each brush in warm water with a drop of shampoo. Rinse brushes thoroughly in cold water, reshape, and place flat on a clean wash cloth to dry.

In this chapter

You discovered tips to find what you need quickly as well as keeping it clean! You were also encouraged to use all of your products up before purchasing more. Applying this one step has made me think twice before purchasing another bottle of fingernail polish or a new type of shampoo – saving me money and significantly reducing my bathroom clutter!

Search me, O God, and know my heart; test me and know my anxious thoughts. Point out anything in me that offends you, and lead me along the path of everlasting life.
~ Psalm 139:23–24

In the next chapter

You will learn how to reclaim both your garage and yard in a weekend! Once that is done you will see how to devise a plan for organizing your garage and yard into use zones, helping you to not only utilize both areas, but to enjoy them too! Don't worry if you aren't able to tackle this right now. If you make a plan it will get done, and don't forget to make some future plans to enhance these areas.

Chapter 12

---~⌒⌒~---

Garage & Yard
Are these areas serving you well?

Scripture

I am the vine; you are the branches. Those who remain in me,
and I in them, will produce much fruit.
For apart from me you can do nothing.
~ John 15:5

In this chapter you will find help in:
- how to reclaim both your garage and yard in a weekend
- devising a plan for organizing your garage and yard into use zones
- utilizing and enjoying both your garage and yard/outside areas
- making future plans to enhance these areas

Have you ever responded to someone by saying, "Just look in the garage"? What is even worse is when you're the one who has to go in there to find something! (I usually find said item as soon as I have replaced it!)

Throughout your personal war against clutter, your garage may have become overloaded with items you have not known what to do with. Take a deep breath, because the time has come to deal with them. You can do this with God's help! Stop right now and ask the Lord for strength, wisdom and joy. There truly is hope for you, even if you never, ever parked your car in your garage. This can be a new experience for both you and your car! We will talk about your yard and outdoor space once we are finished with the garage.

Garage
Ready to start?

Before applying The System (Chapter 1):

- Choose a day to start that will allow you to complete the job; weekends are a good option.
- Devise a plan for where you want to place items that must be stored in your garage.
- Consider purchasing uniform boxes if you have a lot of items you need to store.
- Devise another place for items that you still need but no longer want stored in the garage.
- Decide if you need help — choose your help wisely!
- If you want to involve your family, but not for the whole process, plan to extend your work over a few days. Determine specific aspects of the job, like sorting or hauling items away, for your help to do.
- Crank up some tunes and do whatever you have to do to stay on task, especially if you feel tempted to close the garage door and forget about it. You are going to feel so good when this is finished!
- If you are considering having a garage sale, have it right after you clean out your garage. Otherwise, donate the items to get them out of your garage as soon as possible!

You will not be able to enjoy the satisfaction of a job well done until everything you no longer want is out of there!

Now, apply The System, with some tips and considerations:

- Grab your main garbage can and keep it close for the "throw away" step in applying The System.
- Toss broken items that you know you won't fix. Be realistic; although it might be difficult to toss some items, it will feel so good once you do it.
- Create an area near the door for items that you are going to "give away"; mark with recipient's name.
- Keep in mind how you want to use your garage for the "put away" step in the system: using your garage for storage only, for parking your car(s) and bikes, or for both.

If you use your garage for storage only: mark and organize your boxes so you can easily retrieve what you need. Place the boxes in the back that contain items you do not use regularly, and place the ones that you do in the front. If you have a lot of boxes, make aisles between the stacks, giving you good visibility and access. Boxes: Here is a refresher from Chapter 1 concerning boxes. (If this system is new to you, it bears repeating! If it is not, just skip over and continue to the next section.)

- One of the ways you can identify your boxes is to mark the general contents by category. Indicate the category on each box in the same place using painter's tape. This kind of tape is sold at your home improvement store and is easily removed (usually) without ripping your box.

- Another system is to mark each box with a number. Now mark an index card with the same number, and write the contents of the box on the card, using a pencil. Keep your cards close to the boxes or in a place where they are easily retrieved. When you need to access a particular item, go to your cards and find the number of the box that it is in, and then return it to the marked box. This process is more time-consuming initially, but it will save time and frustration when you no longer have to go through several boxes to find what you need.

I have used this system when paring down my everyday items or when we have been in a temporary living situation.

I was so thankful that I had taken the time to organize our boxes this particular way one year. We were working on our income taxes, and I needed to find a box of documents. I knew the number of the box and was quite excited to lay my hands on exactly what I needed! This has not always been the case.

If you use your garage for parking only, you are the envy of us all!

- Park bikes, scooters, etc., away from your vehicles to protect them from getting scratched!

- Designate where you want bikes parked with colorful tape on your garage floor. (Only use paint if you are sure you will not change that place!)

- Bike racks are helpful in teaching your kids to park their bikes where they are supposed to. Little ones like this!
- A mark on the wall or the infamous tennis ball on a string will help you know how far to pull your car into the garage.

Tips for storage & parking

- Hang bikes from the ceiling to free up more floor space.
- Use shelving on one wall of your garage for storage.
- Designate a shelf for each type of item, like: camping, sports, tools, paint, projects, or work-related items.
- Store and group items on their shelves so they are easily found. Measure so you can use an appropriately sized tub or container. Clear containers are nice for viewing contents; label others.
- If you have a garden shelf, make it a bottom one, where you can store potting soil in a container that allows you to fill a pot directly from it. You will most likely have to sweep up a little dirt, but it will only be on the floor!
- Place large yard tools, like rakes, shovels, etc., in a sturdy garbage can or cylinder.
- A shelf in your garage is a great place to store surplus items you buy in bulk, like paper products, cleaning and laundry products. Instead of carrying them into the house with the rest of your groceries, put these items away right from your car, and decant or refill into smaller sizes from the garage too as you need to. *
- I have an area in my garage that serves as a gift-wrapping center. I use a flat surface to work on, with shelves underneath where I store gift wrap, tissue, and ribbon. I store ribbon from a plastic basket, threading each kind of ribbon through the holes to dispense. Tying your scissors onto a string is a must for a family to ensure they don't go missing! *
- Close to this area is a box that holds gift items I purchase on sale. This makes selecting and wrapping a hostess gift something I can do quickly. *
- If you do not have the time or funds to buy shelving, consider making your own with cinder blocks and lumber, or you could use bookshelves.

* For those of you who live in a climate that will not allow you to use your garage either in summer (because it just gets too hot in there) or in the winter (because it gets too cold), perhaps you can find some space inside the house for these suggestions, if they appeal to you.

Once your garage is clutter-free and you are able to use it at full capacity, you can be on the lookout for specialized shelving, or cabinets or shelves someone is getting rid of. Now pull your car in, if you can, and do a little dance!

Most of the time these seemingly overwhelming jobs aren't that bad once you get started!

Class Comment

Amy, a Your Home Matters class participant, shocked her husband and herself by clearing out and organizing their garage! Her neighbor was her motivation. This neighbor was a single mom, forced to sell her house and short on cash. Amy offered to help her sell some furniture items and to store them in her garage until they sold. Now that she had motivation, she was surprised at how quickly she cleaned out her garage in just one weekend! She not only made space for her neighbor's sale items but organized her husband's work-related things on their own shelves while she was at it!

Maintenance – Keeping it tidy

Unfortunately, our garages are a challenging area to keep under control. Because you have already done the really hard work, it will not take that long to get everything ship-shape again. Throw away the obvious; give away items that you no longer want to friends or to thrift/Goodwill-type stores. Put away everything you are keeping in its designated spot. Unlike in other areas of our home, if items make it to their shelf or area in the garage, that is great. You can always organize each shelf when you have time—or not!

Yard & Outside space

Viewing landscape plans in books and magazines only brought me frustration! Trying to get a landscape plan that would work for us seemed impossible. Our backyard was the challenge: anything we planted would wash out every time it rained! Everything came together when we decided to work with the challenge instead of against it. We created a dry river bed in the natural wash area. That not only solved our problem, we now had a unique feature in our yard. When it rained, the excess water spilled over huge rocks we had placed there and around the river grass we had planted along its edges. We enjoyed this feature so much that we added "the river" to our irrigation system, recycling the water so we could enjoy it even when it wasn't raining. Working with what you have and learning to go with the flow is a concept that is not easy but a good choice and sure to reduce stress.

Ready to start?

You may already have your dream yard, but if not, I hope you will discover how to work with your natural terrain, enhancing what you already have. Even if you are not ready to tackle your whole yard, there are some preliminary things you can do that are fun and will make the job less stressful when you are ready to do more.

Apply The System by throwing away things that are of no use and do not belong in your yard. If this includes weeding, gather the troops, enlisting your family's help! Make this a family project and teach your children that hard work pays off — when they are playing in and enjoying their yard.

Realistically look at the space you have and consider where you could:

- sit and enjoy a cup of coffee or read a book
- play lawn games
- grow a vegetable garden
- grow veggies and herbs in pots
- grow your favorite flowers
- BBQ
- entertain
- provide space for your pets or a dog run
- maybe even put a hot tub

You don't have to be an artist to sketch out your yard. Break it into sections or zones, marking how you would like to use your yard. Work on these zones one at a time, after the overall clean-up is finished, to keep this job manageable.

Survey your neighborhood to scout out plants and trees that you like. This is beneficial if you have moved to a new region so you can see what grows well in your area. If your neighbors wonder what you are doing, let them in on your plan; everyone enjoys having his and her yard admired. You might return home with the names of the plants you like — and maybe even the start of a plant!

The grass is always greener in the other fellow's yard... It seemed like, no matter how hard we worked or how much money we spent, our grass never looked good. This is very frustrating when you are a "do-it-yourselfer" to the core. One of the best decisions we ever made was to get rid of our lawn mower and pay someone else to take care of our grass! This might be a consideration for you too. But if you are determined to get your lawn looking great, ask your neighbors what they use, and you'll finally be on the greener side!

Maintenance – Keeping it tidy and organized

Because yard work is not one of my favorite things, I keep my gloves, clippers and a weed bag in my trunk during the spring and summer. I never really notice the weeds or unruly bushes along our driveway as I leave my home, but upon my return they catch my attention. With these items in my trunk, it takes me just a few minutes to stop to pull weeds and clip roses, etc. Otherwise, I am sure to forget that the area needs my attention. I encourage you to experiment to find what works for you. There is nothing more disheartening than letting your yard become weed- filled and overgrown again!

In this chapter

You received the pep talk (we all need) to declutter and organize your garage and yard! Beforehand planning makes bringing order to these areas a successful endeavor. Don't allow either of these areas to continue to be the cause of stress! Reclaim both your garage and yard for enjoyment! Consider this awesome scripture verse while you are enjoying your yard.

> *I am the vine; you are the branches. Those who remain in me, and I in*
> *them, will produce much fruit. For apart from me you can do nothing.*
> ~ John 15:5

For Your Consideration

In the "entrance" chapter we talked about how inviting the presence of God into our homes is a very wise thing to do. Love, peace and joy are just a few of those life-giving attributes the very presence of God will bring into your life—as well as your home. If you have not invited Jesus into your life, would you consider doing that? He is knocking at the door of your heart and would love to have a relationship with you. This is nothing like "religion," which is man knocking on all kinds of doors trying to reach God. Jesus Christ is the only doorway that leads to God, and relationship with Him will change your life forever!

Please consider the Scriptures and thoughts in this acronym that reminds us that all we need to do is

Believe...

*B*ehold – *I am with you always, to the end of the age.* ~ Matthew 28:20 (ESV) It is nice to know there is someone you can always depend on — God!

*E*veryone *has sinned; we all fall short of God's glorious standard.* ~ Romans 3:23 "Everyone" means everyone; there are no exceptions. *But if we confess our sins to him, he is faithful to forgive us our sins and to cleanse us from all wickedness.* ~ 1 John 1:9

*L*ove – God's love is available for each one of us—and forgiveness too—but it is not automatic; we must believe in Him, with our heart, not just our head. *This is how much God loved the world: He gave his Son, his one and only Son. And this is why: so that no one need be destroyed; by believing in Him, anyone can have a whole and lasting life. God didn't go to all the trouble of sending his Son* *merely to point an accusing finger, telling the world how bad it was. He came to help, to put the world right again. Anyone who trusts in him is acquitted; anyone who refuses to trust him has long since been under the death sentence without knowing it. And why? Because of that person's failure to believe in the one-of-a-kind Son of God when introduced to him.* ~ John 3:16-18 (The Message)

*I*mpossible – It is impossible to come to God any other way than through Jesus. *Jesus told him, "I am the way, the truth, and the life. No one can come to the Father except through me."* ~ John 14:6

*E*verything becomes new – *This means that anyone who belongs to Christ has become a new person. The old life is gone; a new life has begun!* ~ 2 Corinthians 5:17

*V*ictory – *Despite all these things, overwhelming victory is ours through Christ, who loved us.* ~ Romans 8:37

*E*ternity in heaven! If you think the beauty of the earth is amazing, heaven is sure to take your breath away! – *There is more than enough room in my Father's home. If this were not so, would I have told you that I am going to prepare a place for you? When everything is ready, I will come and get you, so that you will always be with me where I am.* ~ John 14: 2-3

It really is quite simple. You can pray, out loud, something like this:

Dear Jesus…
I know you know who I am, but I do not know who you are. My knowledge of you is in my head, not in my heart. I am tired of doing life on my own, and I am inviting you to come into my life. I realize that on my own I cannot please you or even reach you, so I give myself to you forever. I can't wait to experience your love for me and personally know what that looks and feels like.

If you prayed this prayer, I would encourage you to tell someone who also knows Jesus. Remember, we all start at the same place; that confidante will be able to help you grow strong in your faith. I would be honored if you would contact me too! It would be my privilege to pray for you and help you in any way that I can, you can do that at my website: www.suemwilson.com

By the way: "Welcome to the family!"

Love & Blessings,

Sue M. Wilson

Epilogue

You have got to be kidding me—I lived in a garage! Whenever I thought of myself writing a book, I would envision sitting at a lovely desk in a lovely home. "Mindsets" like these seldom turn out as we picture them, and this case was no exception. Writing a curriculum for a class called "*Your Home Matters*," and this book with that same title, was all experienced while living in a garage! I decided not to share this bit of trivia until we were several weeks into the *Your Home Matters* class I was teaching. I thought this rather unusual (even for me) living situation might disqualify me and my expertise.

We built our "shop/garage" and lived there while we were building our home. Now, before you feel too sorry for me, let me try to describe my temporary abode for you. Our living space is about 2200 sq. ft., with two garage doors that roll up. (Those remotes share the coffee table with all the other ones!) We also have a real front door, with a glass transom over the top of it, and a doorbell too! As you enter, the floor is stained concrete, the walls are completely finished inside, just like in a house, with lots of windows. We have a galley kitchen along one wall, with all the appliances any cook would appreciate. Our only room with a door is the bathroom. (Although I am very thankful for the door, I often would appreciate more than just one bathroom!) A free-standing wall was built for our china cabinet on one side and, more important, to provide the closet space we needed on the other side, which is our bedroom. There is a curtain dividing our master bedroom from our guest suite—and, yes, we have had overnight guests! I have to admit that it was fun to create living space without real rooms. Our home looks a little like "loft living" might—or a "furniture store!" We are fortunate that all of our furnishings look good together in these wide open spaces! It certainly makes interesting conversation when someone comes to our home for dinner.

I have come to realize that we all deal with "home matters," no matter where we live. During our garage stay I have taught three "*Your Home Matters*" classes and written the book in your hands. We have made homes in many places, but I have to tell you: I think I am ruined for conventional living — I have come to love and appreciate living in a garage!

From My Heart

Congratulations! You did it! I know that working your way through your home room by room, or in the areas that were stressing you the most, was not an easy task. I sincerely want to tell you that I am proud of you and happy for you, and I hope you had some fun too. I would love to hear about your experiences: the good, the bad, even the ugly—or any tips you are willing to share. I hope you take the opportunity to encourage someone in her or his home matters; an encouraging word goes a long way. If there is any way that I can help you, please do not hesitate to contact me on my web site at **www.suemwilson.com**

P.S. You can also see pictures of my garage there!

Sue M. Wilson

Lavender Valley Photography

Sue Wilson grew up in the Pacific Northwest, but during her forty-plus years of marriage, she and her husband Len have called Canada, Oregon, California and Australia home before putting down roots in North Carolina.

"Little did I know that my favorite childhood book, *The Boxcar Children*, would feed my ingenuity and resourcefulness in someday making anywhere a home. Although I have never lived in an abandoned boxcar, like they did, deep down I knew I could if I had to!"

As custom builders, Sue and Len have enjoyed making beautiful homes from badly neglected ones. They shared these home-making and home-building adventures with their three children and now are watching them — and even some of their nine grandchildren — with pride and pleasure as they set up housekeeping and deal with "home matters" of their own.

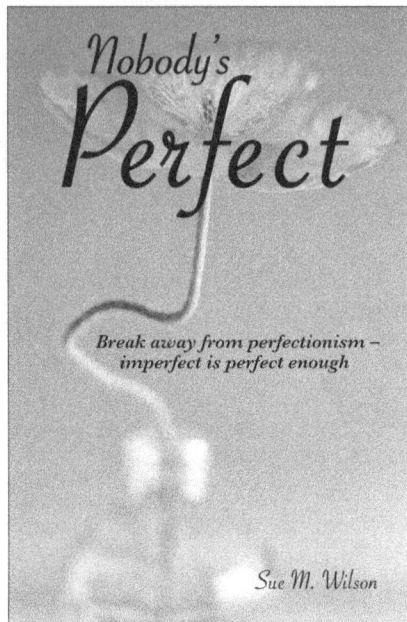

Nobody's
Perfect

*Break away from perfectionism –
imperfect is perfect enough*

Sue M. Wilson

*Sue Wilson is also the author of **Nobody's Perfect.***

Get ready to understand what perfectionism really is – and what it is not! Prepare yourself to completely enjoy how you and your home look as well as being able to enjoy your imperfect relationships – and even your imperfect job!

Nobody's Perfect will equip you to do all of this and more. Even if you don't consider yourself a perfectionist, I'm convinced that all of us have stories to compare and notes to share – a confidence boost we can all use.

Don't live another day feeling like you're not enough, and don't waste another minute comparing yourself to someone else! Don't spend another second holding your personal bar so high that no one can reach it! Begin to discover that your imperfect life is perfect enough – because it is!

www.ingramcontent.com/pod-product-compliance
Lightning Source LLC
Chambersburg PA
CBHW051729040426
42447CB00008B/1048